*TO: Michael,
Hope you enjoy the
book, April Vincent*

INDIAN GIVERS

True Story of Moss Lake

Written by Romey Gallo and Wayne Martin

Wayne Martin

authorHOUSE®

AuthorHouse™
1663 Liberty Drive, Suite 200
Bloomington, IN 47403
www.authorhouse.com
Phone: 1-800-839-8640

© 2009 Romey Gallo and Wayne Martin. All rights reserved.

No part of this book may be reproduced, stored in a retrieval system, or transmitted by any means without the written permission of the author.

First published by AuthorHouse   9/18/2009

ISBN: 978-1-4490-0047-9 (sc)

Printed in the United States of America
Bloomington, Indiana

This book is printed on acid-free paper.

Contents

Chapter 1. The Runnin Gears Of Hell 1

Chapter 2. The Warrior Society 5

Chapter 3. Cowboys And Indians 13

Chapter 4. A Moccasin In The Door 21

Chapter 5. Tears In His Voice 27

Chapter 6. Indian Summer 35

Chapter 7. The Young Vigilantes 41

Chapter 8. Circle The Wagons 51

Chapter 9. Camp Defiance And The Plastic Palace 71

Chapter 10. The Interlopers 77

Chapter 11. Mohawk Women And Children 81

Chapter 12. Salsa In Their Blood 89

Chapter 13. Much Much Wampum 97

Chapter 14. Treaties Or Contracts 105

Chapter 15. Embarrassed District Attorney 111

Chapter 16. Threats Firearms & Firewater 115

Chapter 17. A White Knuckle Night 121

Chapter 18. The Hot Potatoes 129

Chapter 19. Sinister Politicians 139

Chapter 20. Gun-Shy 147

Chapter 21. The Conclusion 153

Acknowledgments

The authors of this book wish to thank the members of COPCA (Concerned Persons of the Central Adirondacks) for their cooperation while we were gathering reference material and conducting interviews for this book. Also thanks to Kyle Blanchfield, Grey Helmerson and Chip Cooper, our resolute editors

Additional thanks to the editors of the various newspapers and the Native Americans of Ganienkeh and others that allowed the re-printing of the many photographs used:
Utica Observor Dispatch
Watertown Times
Rome Daily Sentinal
Boonville Herald
Montreal Star
Steve Charzuk, State Police Photographer
Fingerlakes Times
Old Forge Historical Society
Woodgate Library

A special Thanks to MaryBeth Scalzo and Chief Lous Hall. Their combined artistic talents were used to design our cover. MaryBeth is responsible for the wampum belt and Chief Hall for the sketch of the Native American busts.

And Lastly, a very special thanks to our wives, Elaine and Marcia, for their patience and understanding. Without that type of cooperation this book would have been impossible to write.

All royalties obtained after initial cost of this book will be given to the non-profit organization of Top Cat, Surf City, N.C. This organization traps feral cats and kittens, neuters and spays the animals and performs necessary medical care. It is also a non kill organization.

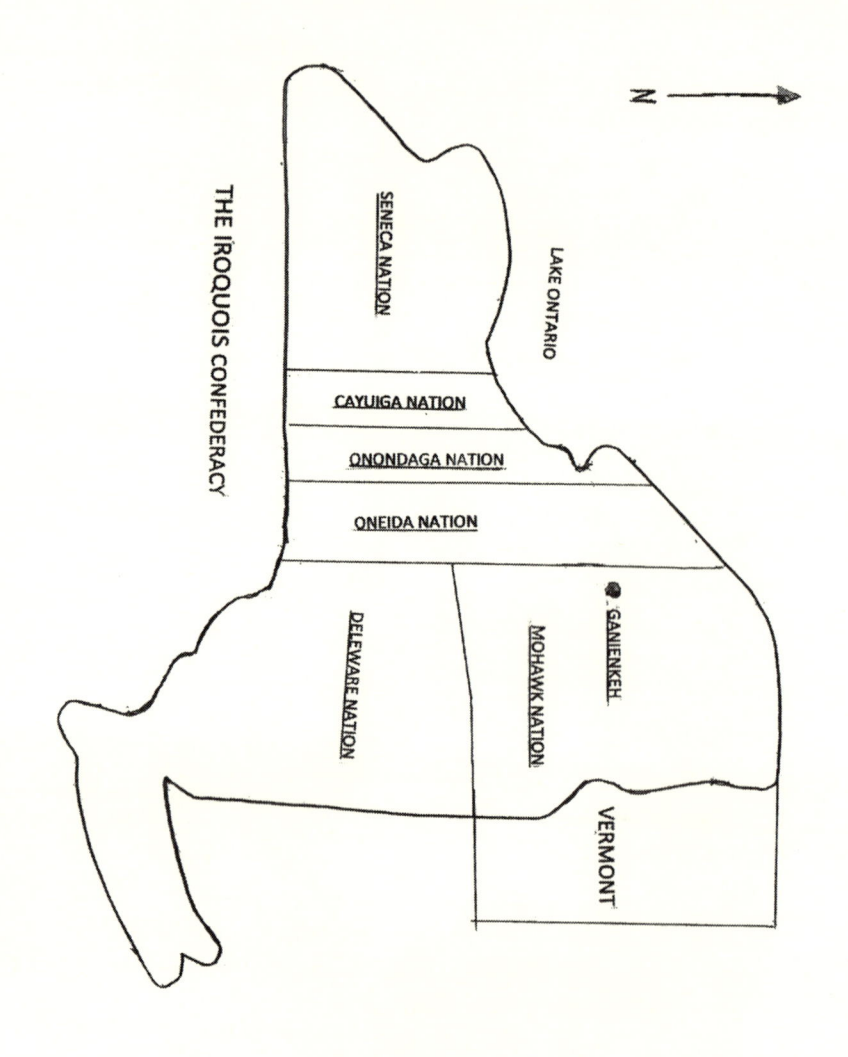

THE IROQUOIS CONFEDERACY

SENECA NATION

CAYUGA NATION

ONONDAGA NATION

ONEIDA NATION

DELEWARE NATION

MOHAWK NATION

GANIENKEH

LAKE ONTARIO

VERMONT

N →

LOCATION OF GANIENKEH IN NEW YORK STATE

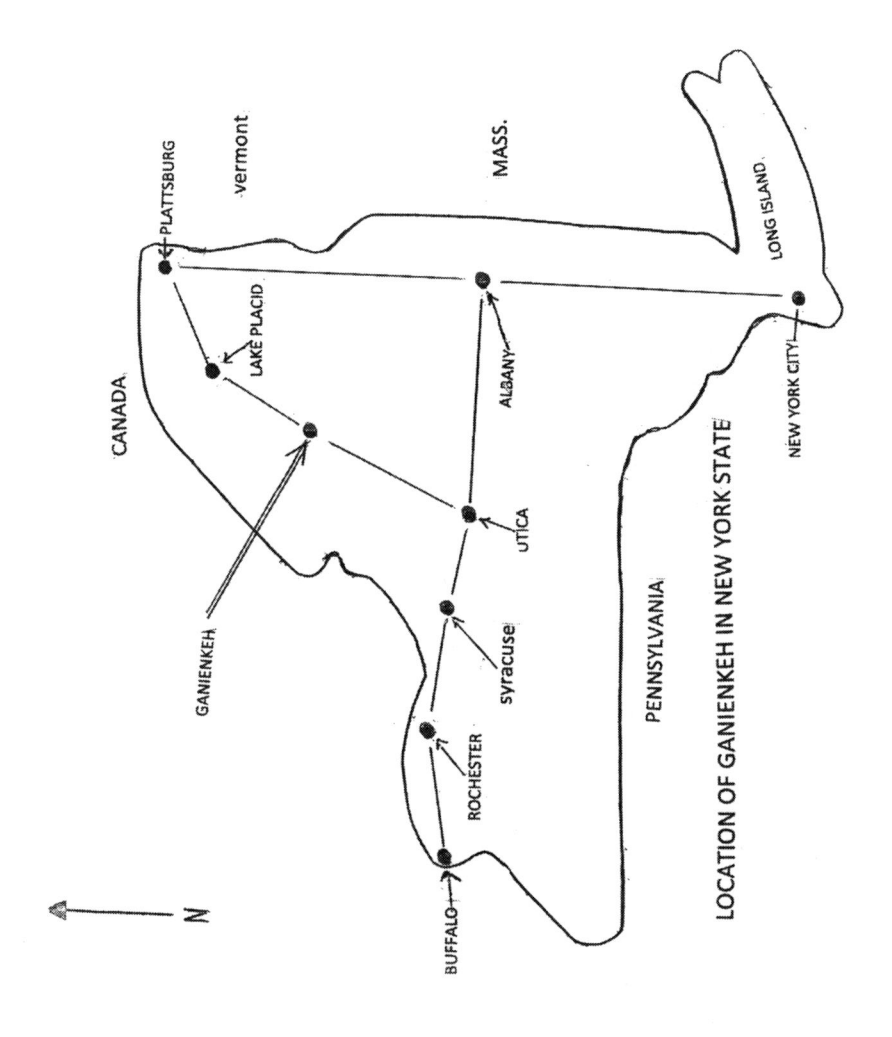

MOSS LAKE & GANIENKEH AREA

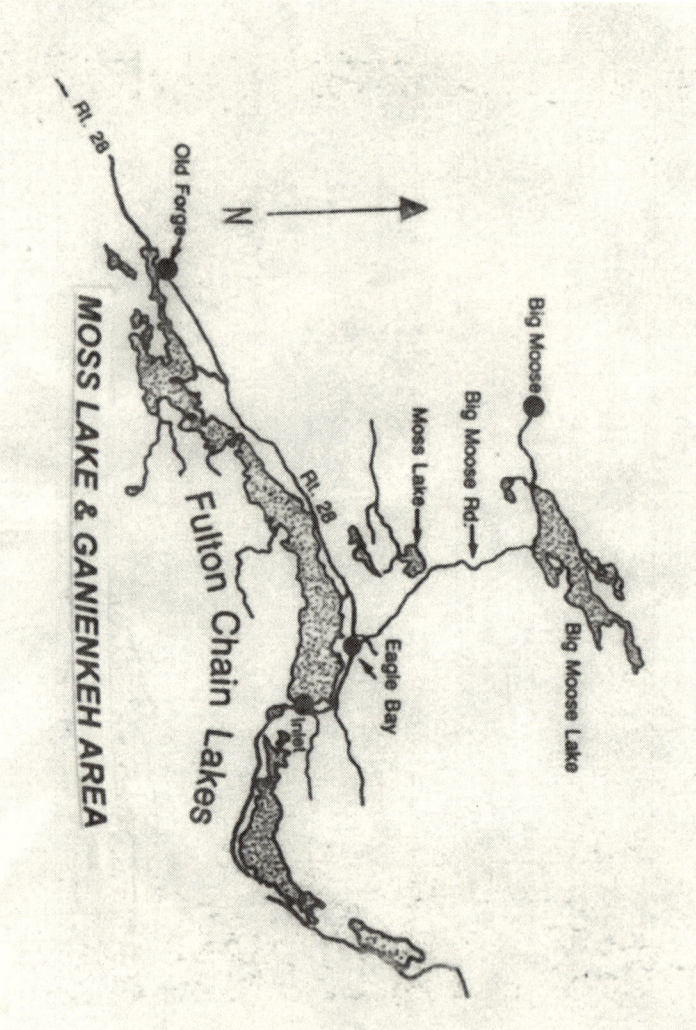

Time Line

JULY 1968 -Formation of the American Indian Movement
FEBRUARY 1973 -Wounded Knee erupts—
SUMMER 1973 -Warriors first act - Attempt to cleanse Caughnawaga Res.
SUMMER & FALL 1973 -Plan to invade N.Y. State is hatched -
APRIL 1974 -Mohawks repossess Moss Lake
APRIL 1974 —Indians advise they own most of upstate NY and Vermont
SUMMER 1974 -Indians plea for sustenance
SUMMER 1974 -Vigilante activity strong
SUMMER & FALL-Harassment intensifies
OCTOBER 28, 1974 -Madigan & Drake shot by Warriors
OCTOBER 28,1974 -State Police go into action
OCTOBER 29,1974 -Negotiations begin
NOVEMBER 1974 -Concerned Persons of the Central Adirondacks (COPCA) is formed
NOVEMBER 1974 - Interlopers arrive to defend Ganienkeh

DECEMBER 1974 -Aprile Madigan goes home
WINTER 1975 - Lawsuits against State are filed by Drake and Madigan
WINTER 1975 - Lawsuit to evict Indians
JULY 1975 -DEC enlarges land held by Mohawks 1975
SRING 1975 - COPCA hires Michael Blair as Spokesman
SPRING 75 thru 1978 Blair
Enters into debates with Mohawks
AUGUST 1976 - Everett Report is discovered and Taken to negotiators
JULY 1976 -Arrest of Stone Hawk Goeman
SUMMER 1976 - info that a Trooper will be killed -
FALL 1976 - Possible attempt on Troopers life
FALL 1976- Blair discovers feds and State knew of Indian takeover
JULY 25,1977 -Turtle Island Trust Agreement is made
FALL 1978 -Mohawks go to Town of Altona, St. Lawrence County

Preface

No doubt, many today have heard of the demeaning term, "Indian Giver," which appears to be an unfair stereotype of the first inhabitants on our continent. One who gives a gift and later takes it back, as though they, the Indians, do not keep their word. (Wikipedia On-line dictionary) History doesn't clear up the true origin of this phrase or its meaning. Although many historians believe this was the aboriginals' way of barter. If they did not like a deal they had entered, they would take their property back and return the other party's merchandise. There is, however, another likely explanation for the idiom; some historians believe that it may reflect the many broken promises made to the American Indian by the White Man: the land and other resources given to the aborigine by treaty, which, when these resources became valuable, were taken back by the whites (hence Indian Giver). Many historians now agree that where deceit was concerned the settlers far out distanced the American Indian. They further agree that it is custom for the conqueror to make the conquered out to be dishonest and stupid, which is how negative stereotypes like "Indian Giver" often come into existence.

This book presents another definition of "Indian Giver," one in which the giver is the State of New York and/or the Federal Government giving to the Mohawk Warrior Society in a possible effort to solve one political problem with another political problem: the Mohawk Indian incursion of Moss Lake.

The story line follows closely the events of the Indian takeover of a piece of land owned by New York State, located in the Adirondack Mountains. In 1974, the Warriors Society, a group of Canadian Mohawks, came down from Canada along with a few Indians from the Akwesasne Territory (U.S. side of Canadian border), and by the threat of force, took over and occupied a six hundred twelve acre abandoned girls' camp called Moss Lake. The Mohawks argue that the takeover was really a repossession of land taken from them illegally by the government as result of the Joseph Brandt Treaty of 1797, which has become the basis for the Mohawk's many claims against the State of New York for the return of nine million acres of New York State and Vermont.

One could argue that this incursion was in fact an invasion of the United States as the Mohawks considered themselves a sovereign nation at that time. However it seemed that the takeover was dismissed as nothing by both the State and Federal Government. Many believed that this position was taken in an effort to downplay the magnitude of the whole event, hoping it would just go away, but perhaps there was a more sinister reason, one we will explore in the pages that follow.

The three year occupation of Moss Lake resulted in a major rift between the Warrior Society, the State of New York and Concerned Citizens of the Central Adirondacks (COPCA). The Federal Government kept a very low profile and would not admit publicly that they were involved in any way. Before it was over bloodshed, shootings, harassment and political turmoil occurred on a regular basis. The Indian occupation was considered a ruse and attempted extortion by the White's of the area. COPCA believed that the Indians really didn't care about the small girls' camp, which was agriculturally unsound. They wanted "big game" wherein they could establish their true Ganienkeh (Gun-yung-gay) which means the land of flint in Iroquois. Several lawsuits were filed from all sides of the dispute, including an attempt by the State to have the courts issue an eviction notice for the removal of the Mohawk Indians. The Native Americans made complaints to President Gerald Ford and to the United Nations concerning the harassment they were receiving and the constant attempt by the State to assert its jurisdiction. Some White groups and churches sided with the Indians, providing moral support and financial aid. The State Police (Troopers) became mediators between the parties involved and were not allowed to enforce the laws with regard to the Native Americans. The assignment as buffers resulted in thousands of hours of Trooper time expended on this matter at a great cost to the State.

After several shootings, one of which wounded a little girl and a local man, the State began negotiations in earnest to solve this festering problem. After almost three years of negotiations, it appeared that everyone became a winner except the local people (COPCA) who lived in the area and, of course the victims of the shootings. The Indians were relocated on 698 acres in the Town of Altona, Clinton County, of upper New York State. Additionally, the "Turtle Island Trust" was established in Clinton County giving the Indians exclusive use of 5,700 acres of land. Clearly a precedent was set by the negotiations which would have an everlasting effect on the future. The outcome of the Moss Lake event can be seen in each and every negotiation between the States and the American Indian since that time.

To this day feelings run deep amongst the white population of the area, who view the State as being weak for failing to evict the Indians and giving in to their demands. The whites now realize that the Indians used them to stir the pot when things got too quiet, putting additional pressure on the State to settle this dispute. It was a time when, perhaps for the first time, Troopers were not allowed to enforce the law, feeling the impact of a political system, that only recently dealt with the carnage of the Attica Prison Riot, where much bloodshed occurred at the hands of the State Troopers, called in to quell the riot and hostage taking.

The approach of this book to the issues and events that occurred is not scholarly but a straight forward mission of facts as seen through the eyes of two State Police Supervisors who were there and deeply involved in the happenings as they unfolded. The reader must make up his own mind in this matter, weighing the evidence, the beliefs of all parties, and the eventual outcome. Hopefully the issues have been presented fairly, as the utmost care has been taken to ensure all involved obtain a fair shake. With the neutral approach taken, we have tried to respect the opinions of all sides, with account taken of what was experienced by the authors. If investigation of a particular issue indicated that it was most likely accurate then opinions of the writers concerning that matter are included.

Chapter 1

The Runnin Gears Of Hell

The Adirondack Park lies in the northernmost portion of New York State, just to the south of the Canadian border. It is the largest track of unspoiled wilderness east of the Mississippi River. It is comprised of millions of acres of timber, almost all of which could be categorized as wilderness. This great forest is populated by big game, i.e. white tail deer, black bear, wolves, coyotes, bobcats, and the occasional moose that wanders in from Maine or Canada when the St. Lawrence River freezes over during particularly cold winters. Most of the smaller species of animals and birds indigenous to the New England States also inhabit this pristine area. The animals far outnumber the human population, comprised mostly of hunters, campers and hikers. In the winter, large amounts of snowfall lure snowmobile enthusiasts from all over the United States to this frosty playground. A spattering of year round residents remains mostly in and around a few small hamlets.

Pristine lakes are everywhere, the largest of these being Lake George, Lake Placid, Saranac and Raquette Lake. The Fulton Chain of Lakes starts in Old Forge, a year round tourist mecca, and heads northeast. They are called 1st Lake, then 2nd Lake, on through to 8th Lake, just to the southwest of Raquette Lake. All of these lakes are inhabited by various species of trout and provide warm weather activities such as water sports, canoeing, sailing, and fishing. In the winter the frozen lakes are occupied by ice fishermen, skiers, skaters and snowmobile enthusiasts. State Route 28 winds its way northeasterly along the northern shores of the chain. It then passes through the tiny hamlet of

Eagle Bay where if one should turn left onto the Big Moose Road, and travel north, he or she would enter one of the most remote wilderness areas of the Adirondack Mountains. The road is a patchwork quilt of macadam, very bumpy and narrow. About two miles in, the road goes through the Moss Lake Girls' Camp. Continuing on, one would see the road turn to dirt at Big Moose in the area of Carter Station. It is hardly traversable for the next ten to twelve miles, until it reaches the hamlet of Stillwater. Everything about the area spells adventure and intrigue, but nothing, more than Big Moose Lake itself.

The name, "Big Moose Lake" congers up mystery and wonder to those who have heard, or wish to hear of its history. Things that have happened there lend credence to the stories and tales of the area. In the late eighteen hundredths the Glenmore Hotel was built. Then in 1903, the Big Moose Inn was erected, both on the southern end of the lake. They remain much the same today as then. During their visits, adventurers and thrill seekers travel this poorly maintained road to enjoy the food and storytelling at the restaurants (hotels) of things explained and unexplained. Theodore Drieser used the Lake's murder mystery as the basis for his renowned book, An American Tragedy, published in 1925. It was the true life story of Chester Gillette, a young man of promised wealth and stature. One of his girlfriends, Grace Brown, became pregnant. She was of lesser social status than Chester and stood in the way of his prosperity. Filled with fear, he plotted her murder at Big Moose Lake. He took Grace to the lake, she believing they were going there to marry. The couple stayed at the Glenmore Hotel in Big Moose and departed on a rowboat outing the following morning, neither returned to the Inn that evening. The following day, Grace's body was found on the bottom of the lake. There were lacerations to her face and scalp. Chester escaped on foot through the wilderness, only to eventually be caught and charged with murder. He was found guilty by jury trial in Herkimer County and executed by electrocution.

To this day, stories and theories abound concerning the murder. It is said by many that Grace's spirit haunts the lake and its surrounding buildings. Her ghostly image has been reported by credible witnesses, seen both in the lake's camps, and on the water. The repeated sightings and growing interests have resulted in many media events concerning this mystery. Such as a 1988 PBS special, "Murder at Big Moose Lake," a 1996 episode of Unsolved Mysteries, "Grace's Ghost," and a 1997 History Channel special, "Crime In Time."

And, so it was, that the Madigan family, Roger and Jean, of Geneva, New York, and their two children, Steven and Aprile, traveled into this remote area to experience adventure and intrigue during their vacation in late October 1974. They enjoyed dinner at the Glenmore Hotel, where the patrons almost always discuss the Grace Brown murder in detail for visitors, including her ghostly appearances on the lake. The stage was set for a long lonely ride back through the wilderness on a very dark and scary road.

Their vehicle slowly headed south towards the hamlet of Eagle Bay. The children were now anxious to return to civilization as things had become scary to them. They were unaware of what was lurking around the next bend in the road. As the car reached the abandoned Moss Lake Girls' Camp, automatic gunfire erupted. Bullets of military caliber smacked into and through the car, penetrating the metal as though it were paper. Glass was flying, bullets ricocheting through the car. Everyone was screaming as Roger accelerated, hoping to get his family through whatever it was that was happening. When it was over, little nine year old, Aprile, laid on the back seat crying, blood running down her side. "Daddy I think I'm going to die," were her words. Later, a local resident was heard to say, "It must have been like the runnin' gears of hell."

Chapter 2

The Warrior Society

Somewhere in the Kanawake Indian territory located just to the north of the United States border with Canada, ten men and ten women sat at a dimly lit table. Three kerosene lanterns lit the room, casting their shadows against the wall. Their dress was traditional 20th century White Man's garb: no war bonnets, no feathers, and no buckskin. Also absent were the traditional counsel fire, the sound of drums in the background, and the medicine man. No drugs or alcohol were in sight. In the bygone days of Cochise, Crazy Horse, and Sitting Bull, many of these symbols were used to incite the warriors before battle, particularly the "War Dance." However, there was no need for motivation at this Mohawk's counsel setting. The men and women needed no prodding. There was no laughter, but plenty of anger expressed on their faces.

This was the Mohawk Nation's Warrior Society, also known as the "Long House People." Some of these men were considered dangerous and wanted by the U.S. and/or Canadian governments. Some were participants in the 1973 Wounded Knee insurrection in South Dakota. These men and women had broken off ties with the Tribal Nations (the Iroquois and non-traditional Mohawks) who felt the Warriors were becoming much too militant and did not condone their planned "takeover" of some New York State Land. This gathering was their final meeting before their armed invasion, emphatically called "repossession" by the Warriors, of the Moss Lake Girls' Camp in the Adirondack Mountains of New York. To the Indians, this was their land "The Land of Flint," and the home of the legendary Warrior of the Onondaga's,

Hiawatha, or "Hiawentha" according to the Mohawk people. He had named the land "the land of flint", no doubt because flint, a natural occurring stone in the area, was used to produce sparks when struck by an abrasive and the source for starting fires for the Indians.

The Warriors first used some of their newly found power in 1973, when they flexed their muscles and tried to evict one thousand people from the Caughnawaga reservation (later called Kanawake), just to the south of Montreal and north of the U.S. Canadian border. The non-Indians, as the Warriors described them, whom they sought to evict, were, in fact recognized as Mohawks by the Canadian Government. The "Nons", whom the Warrior Society referred to as "Paper Indians," were accused of taking the jobs and businesses of the "traditional" and were enjoying the many rights of the true Mohawk Indian, such as tax free living. (Akwesasne Notes 1973)

The Warriors took it upon themselves to cleanse the reservation, but the Tribal Chief's balked and called the Provincial Police. Seven Warriors were arrested, but eventually released, after approximately one hundred additional traditionalists (Warrior sympathizers) came to their aid. The police were run off on foot, mainly because their cars had been overturned, and the officers clubbed. They later returned with reinforcements to provide police protection to the reservation and to attempt to dislodge the remaining warriors holed up in a long house along with Chief Louis Hall (Karoniakajeh). The Warriors realized they were fighting their own people and needed to turn their focus on those who they felt had stolen their land. That night, the conspiracy to invade the U.S. and the State of New York was born. After a few days of negotiation with the Canadian government, the remainders of the warriors were dislodged by the Provincial Police. (Montreal Star 1973)

The warriors needed a location that they could easily take and defend, should the government learn of the incursion and decide to take it back at a later date. Without the knowledge of the locals, the Indian scouts actually entered the Moss Lake Girls' Camp in the Adirondack Mountains of New York State, to inventory the buildings for their planning. Some believed that the Mohawks also had help in finding the best location for their plans, perhaps from a local sympathizer.

This group of Mohawks felt that the Canadian and U.S. governments ignored them, while, nonetheless, catering to and negotiating with other Indian Nations. Their repossession would make all sit up and take notice that they too were downtrodden Native Americans. Their list of grievances was long, to say the least, but, most importantly, they wished to repossess the land of their ancestors which they claimed the White Man had stolen from them. They believed that nine million acres of upper New York State and Vermont really belonged to the Mohawks who were part of the Six Nation Confederacy of the Iroquois (the Mohawks, the Oneidas, the Onondagas, the Cayugas, the Senecas and the Tuscaroras). They argued that the United States Government and New York State had taken the Mohawk portion illegally. It was their contention that the Canandaigua Treaty of 1794 with the U.S. government guaranteed that they, the Mohawks, were the owners of most of upper New York State and Vermont. They further claimed that the Joseph Brandt treaty of 1797, that allegedly sold this land back to New York State for $1,000, was illegal. According to these Mohawks, Brandt did not have the authority to sell Mohawk land, as he was not a true chief. To be legal, all chiefs of the confederacy had to sign the document. In addition, the original document was made between the United States and the Six Nations, and the State of New York could not be party to this transaction as the U.S. Constitution forbade the States to negotiate with sovereign nations. The Indians believed that this fact also made the Brandt Treaty invalid. They further believed that the Treaties made in 1784 (Fort Stanwick) and 1789 (Fort Harmer), set boundary lines between the whites and the Indians and established the Iroquois as a sovereign nation.

The Mohawks intended to occupy the Moss Lake Girls' Camp until the State of New York relinquished a more desirable prize (many more acres of agricultural land) where they could establish the true "Ganienkeh." They wanted their own sovereignty where they could govern themselves and establish their own ideals without the influence or mandates of the White Man or other Indian Nations. They would re-learn how to become self-sufficient, not having to ride on the shoulders of other people, Indian Nations, and the White Man. They would possess no alcohol or drugs, living environmentally green at Ganienkeh and in accord with the Great Law (Gayanerakowa). The Indians described this Great Law as the Iroquois Constitution, said to be the first of its kind in the world and copied by the White man. But, most of all, they wanted the rest of the world to understand what they were trying to accomplish. Their plan was not to repossess private property, but public property, and to avoid bloodshed while doing it. Their leaders were Chief Louis Hall (Karoniaktajeh), Sub Chief Jake Swamp, and Arthur Montour (Kakwirakeron), who was the Mohawks' charismatic spokesperson. Also, there were Richard "Cartoon" Alfred, (a direct descendent of legendary Shawnee leader Tecumseh), Paul Deleronde, and select Mohawk men and women. The soles of their moccasins may have been worn but their souls within became re-nourished knowing of what their future could bring.

According to the book "Like A Hurricane" by Smith and Warrior, their plan was inspired by the formation of the American Indian Movement (AIM), in Minneapolis, Minnesota, in July 1968. The three main activists were: Clyde Bellecort, Dennis Banks, and George Mitchell. They were all from the Ojibwa nation. The goal was to unite all Indian Nations into one cohesive movement, against the perceived repression and aggression of the United States. They got their first big assignment when called by the Oglala Sioux on February 27, 1973. Sarah Bad Heart Bull's son had been stabbed and murdered by a White man, Darle Smitz in the town of Custer, just to the east of the Pine Ridge Reservation. He was released the same day on a very small amount of bail (five thousand dollar bond) and later charged with second-degree manslaughter. The traditionals felt that there were two sets of standards and the light treatment dealt to Whites was tacit approval of violence against the Indian people. AIM agreed to help.

The Oglala Sioux Indians that resided on the Wounded Knee Reservation, believed that most of their treaties with the United States (three hundred seventy one) had been broken. They were being pushed onto smaller reservations, with less and less employment, income, health care and education. Their fight was also with the United States Government's sanctioned Goon Squad who carried out the desires of the Bureau of Indian Affairs (BIA), an arm of the U.S. government. The traditionals accused Dickie Wilson's Goon Squad, who represented the non-traditionals of escalating violence against them. They cited another severe problem; strip mining on the Pine Ridge Reservation. The sanctioned government by the BIA encouraged the sale of these mountains to prospectors for mining. The Black Hills, which were owned by the Lakota Sioux, surrounded the Pine Ridge Reservation which encompassed the Wounded Knee area. People were beginning to see the effects of chemicals in their water (birth defects, sick children). The Lakota Nation was split and violent confrontations began to escalate at Wounded Knee.

On July 8, 1970, in a message to Congress, President Nixon added fuel to the American Indian's fire by stating: "The first Americans- the Indians- are the most deprived group in our nation. On virtually every scale of measurement- employment, income, education, health - the conditions of the Indian people rank at the bottom. This condition is the heritage of centuries of injustice... The American Indians have been oppressed and brutalized, deprived of their ancestral lands and denied the opportunity to control their own destiny." (Ganienkeh Manifesto 1974)

Nixon's words and the American Indian Movement (AIM) fanned a fire that had been smoldering for decades over the manner in which the American Indian was being treated by the United States. This resulted in small takeovers and occupations all over the country such as the incursion of Alcatraz Island by members of AIM, which was quickly put down by the government. These outbursts were mostly insignificant, but then Wounded Knee erupted. Compared to the prior incidents, this event was like Mount Saint Helen's rumbling. It was 1973 when the Pine Ridge Reservation in South Dakota became an inferno. Indians from all over the United States traveled to the Village of Wounded Knee in protest of the Fort Laramie Treaty, which they felt had once again been broken by the government over many issues.

If, at first the U.S. government had ignored the protest, it may have just gone away without disclosure to the press. But the U.S. responded with overwhelming force, bringing national media coverage to the matter. The might of the U.S. military was brought in and surrounded the reservation in an apparent effort to intimidate the Indians into surrender. Present were: the Federal Bureau of Investigation (FBI), Drug Enforcement Agency (DEA), Bureau of Indian Affairs (BIA), Alcohol Tobacco and Firearms (ATF), Marshals, State Police, and Local Police. For seventy one days the Indians and the government battled, with thousands of rounds of small caliber weaponry exchanged. When the two sides finally put down their weapons on May 4, 1973, two F.B.I. agents were wounded and two Indians were dead. The Nixon White House promised that the Fort Laramie Treaty would be re-visited if the Indians would lay down their weapons. That treaty of 1880 primarily gave the Black Hills to the Lakota's, but as time went on, prospectors looking for gold encroached and the land was being strip mined.

The Indian Chiefs agreed to the cease-fire, hoping they had finally gotten the attention of the United States Government and believing they had the President's sympathy, based on his July 8, 1970 statement. But, more than one hundred fifty Indians escaped with their weapons, probably because they did not trust Washington. Somehow the escaping Indians breached the roadblocks and the watchful eyes of the agents surrounding them.

The White House immediately broke the cease-fire agreement, President Nixon declaring that the government would not negotiate with "Any American Indian," a complete reversal of his statement made on July 8, 1970. As result of the Wounded Knee Occupation, over seven hundred indictments were handed down by the Government, and many Indians fled to Canada to avoid prosecution. (Revolutionary Worker #952.)

In the 1973 March issue of Time Magazine, a clue emerged as to the effect the Wounded Knee Occupation had on the American Indian. "Wounded Knee has been a catalyst" says Donald White, an Oneida Indian who was a student at the University of Illinois. 'We have been apathetic for too many years. The people out there (Wounded Knee) are willing to die for us, maybe it's time to do something too.' Many other Indians, particularly the young, echo his sentiments." (Time Magazine 3/19/73).

This catalyst effect brought in a new era, which gave life to the Mohawk Nation's most recent Warrior Society at the Caughnawaga Territory. The Mohawk Counsel of Chiefs approved of the Warriors Society, not realizing or believing that the new power given to the Warriors could get out of hand. The Warriors first action was the attempted cleansing of the Caughnawaga Reservation of non-Indians, resulted in failure. This action was the spark that gave thought to the takeover of Moss Lake.

In an effort to justify their actions at Kanawake, and later at Moss Lake, the Warrior Society pointed to the Great Law (Gayanerakowa) from which they derive their authority and power. Within the Great Law's words, the War Chief and his men are created and given certain powers and mandates that they must follow. Louis Hall, (Karoniaktajeh) the Chief of the Warriors at the time of the Moss Lake takeover, defined the Warrior Society and its charges as follows: "The Great Law (Gayanerakowa) called them the War Chief and his men. The term Warrior Society was given by the White Man. It seems to fit nicely. The Great Law has definite functions for the War Chief and his men. They are charged with the defense and protection of the people. Their duties may take many forms: keeping the peace, teaching, public speaking, repossessing lost lands and human rights, taking care of confrontations, settling dangerous disputes and international negotiations, and doing work of all kinds to promote the welfare of the people" (Louis Hall, Warrior Society newsletter, Moss Lake 1974).

The duties and mandates of the Great Law and the interpretation given to it by Louis Hall, likened it to the Whiteman's police, military, judge and jury with regard to Indian affairs. The Warriors had been given a great deal of power without any checks and balances to regulate their activities. The Mohawk Nation was unable to control them and did not condone the planned takeover of the Moss Lake Girls' Camp in New York State, but was without power to stop them. The Chiefs felt that the State would vigorously oppose this action and many would die and/or be injured. After the incursion was complete, and no confrontations with the State had taken place, the Mohawk Nation took a deep breath and sanctioned the movement.

The Chief, Louis Hall, in an Indian Survival crisis Newsletter wrote: "In the Iroquois way, every man is a warrior - lately, the girls and even the older women have demanded instructions in the art of the Warriors, handling guns, etc. They mean to have a part in any future armed struggles for survival." This was Hall's way of saying "atta boy" and "atta girl" to boost the morale of his Warrior Society and to bring back the Traditional way, no matter what the cost.

*Pictured: First Sergeant Romaine B. Gallo early
on in his career as a young State Trooper.*

Chapter 3

Cowboys And Indians

The phone rang in the Zone Sergeant's office at State Police New Hartford, the Zone Headquarters of Zone One, Troop "D." The desk man hollered to Zone Sergeant Romey Gallo, a fourteen year veteran police officer, "It's the Captain for you, it sounds important." Gallo was the acting Zone Commander that evening and had hoped to spend the shift doing paper work and reviewing investigative reports.

The New York State Police are the primary full police service in New York State. There are ten Troops within the State, broken down by zones, usually two or three per Troop. Zones typically cover two or three counties, further divided by substations, which are strategically positioned for maximum coverage. Division Headquarters and the Academy are located in Albany. This was the configuration of the division in 1974.

Some counties of the State had active Sheriff's Departments that could assist with police matters, and some townships had developed Town Police. Depending upon the time of year and day, the nearest backup for a Trooper could be fifty some miles away, particularly so, in the rural reaches of the State. Troopers learned to function without the privilege of constant support and supervision and the word "backup" wasn't in their vocabulary. Yet, the police work got done with little need for the use of force. Their reputation for toughness when needed and enforcement of all State laws by the fair import of the law, made their work much easier.

On the phone, the captain's voice was not his usual jovial George Chromey, but stern and all business. From the initial greeting it was apparent something serious was happening. Troop "B," the Troop to the north of Troop "D," had developed intelligence that a group of Canadian Mohawk Indians were mounting a caravan of automobiles loaded with braves, women and children, supplies and weapons. The reported goal was to take over a piece of State land somewhere in Herkimer or Hamilton Counties. A Troop "B" officer was detailed to tail them as they entered the State from Canada, crossing into the U.S. through the Plattsburgh Customs. The information indicated that the Indians would use force, if necessary, to accomplish their takeover. Their exact numbers were unknown, but there was no doubt they would be heavily armed and use whatever force was necessary to achieve their goal. Both officers recalled the Wounded Knee fiasco just months earlier, and dreaded the thought of such an occurrence in New York State.

A case of this magnitude would most likely be presented to the Governor, who would, in turn, seek counsel from the Federal Government. A decision could take three or more hours. Gallo was instructed to head into the area of upper Herkimer County within the Adirondack Park, but to take no action except gathering intelligence until further advised. He knew he should plan for the possibility of an order coming down to defend the abandoned Moss Lake Girls Camp, which was the State land that seemed most desirable for the Indians. There was, however, a second option to consider defending: The Moose River Plains.

The Moss Lake Girls' Camp, in the town of Webb, Herkimer County, seemed the most logical goal for the Indians. It had old buildings that would provide shelter from the elements, which, in the Mountains, could be very cruel. Temperatures of forty and fifty below zero were not unusual during winter. Blizzards occurred regularly with as much as six feet of snow on the level. How would they survive during the winter months? Gallo wondered.

The camp, recently abandoned, had been built for summertime use only, for girls of the elite from New York City. The other location in the mountains, the Moose River Plains, was also a concern. It had few buildings and was even more remote then Moss Lake. One road to

Indian Givers

each made either one defendable from within by the Troopers, or by the Indians, whoever got there first.

The head of a well to do family during the time the Moss Lake Girls' Camp was in operation (1920 thru 1970), probably would want to send his teenage daughter there for the summer. Girls from the upper crust of New York City as well as girls from all over the U.S. came to the camp to experience the various outdoor activities such as horseback riding, fencing, boating, swimming, canoeing, etc.. It was known during those times as the most prestigious camp in the Nation. The lake located within the camp property is a small, pristine lake on the westerly side of the Big Moose Road in the Township of Webb, Herkimer County. During Civil War time it was known as Whipple Lake. Then, during the 70's, it evolved into Morse Lake, then eventually into Moss Lake. The acidic soil surrounding the lake made for beautiful green moss. No doubt this was the reason it was called Moss Lake. In 1919, George Longstaff purchased the 612 acres to fulfill his dream of building a girls' camp there. His creation turned out to be a jewel of the central Adirondacks. Eventually the camp was sold to Robert and Jane Riders. In 1972 the Rider's sold the camp to the Nature Conservancy who later sold it to New York State. It then fell under the jurisdiction of the Department of Environmental Conservation (DEC).

Gallo's unmarked police car was loaded with three Ithaca twelve gauge shotguns, five boxes of slugs and five boxes of double O buckshot. The trunk was filled with several extra cartons of flares, first aid equipment, fire extinguishers, ropes and emergency lighting. The officer had worn his bullet proof vest various times before and hated its discomfort. This time it gave him a feeling of warmth and security. He had sixty five miles to travel to reach the area of concern, up Route 12 to the north, then northeast on Route 28 into the area of the chain of lakes. The time would be well spent going over the many scenarios that could develop, should the order come to defend the State property. He would be the officer in charge at the scene. What would he do if? Wounded Knee was always in the back of his mind, the dead Indians and the wounded agents. Gallo realized that he only had six or seven troopers that could be pulled from their stations in the zone, without reaching into those that were off duty. The other on-duty members would be needed to provide coverage in their respective station areas.

An occasional glance at the work schedule lying on the seat beside him did not yield any additional manpower as he had hoped. However, he knew that if the higher ups decided to stop the Mohawks, the Town of Webb Police Department could be counted on to assist and could be quickly mobilized into action. Chief of Police, Bob Crofoot, was a close friend of the State Police and would assist if requested. A trooper from State Police Remsen was sent to team up with Chief Crofoot at about 5:00 p.m... Their objective would be to check all campsites in the area for evidence of the Mohawk's moving in. Much to their surprise, some of the area businessmen already knew of the possible Indian takeover. But how did they know? The State Police learned of the possible Indian plans only minutes earlier. Gallo and Crofoot agreed that the Chief could conduct that investigation at a later time, in an effort to shed light on this very strange development. There was no time for it now.

For several miles of the trip, the officer recalled events and stories of his childhood about Indians. Particularly, Cowboys and Indians, a game played with his boyhood friends and brothers that involved the making of bows and arrows that they would whittle from small branches and trees. He recalled stories and movies of Indians slaughtering white folks, burning their homes and scalping the grownups, while the children were whisked away to live in the wilderness with their captors. He was very much aware that most of this portrayal was the overblown imaginings of writers, but it did add to the anxiety he was feeling. After all, it could be the real "Cowboys and Indians" this night. Chills went down his spine, and throughout his body, as he realized the magnitude of what he was heading into could rest firmly on his shoulders.

Now was the time to weigh each plan and determine the best for the situation, one in which no one would be injured or killed. If the order came to stop the takeover, it would be dark by that time and the Indians would be filtering in all night. There were a few street lights on the Big Moose Road at the edge of the Hamlet of Eagle Bay: a great place for a roadblock. There were also plenty of big trees that could be easily felled across the roadway. The Indians would be traveling with their women and children, and perhaps they would have babies on board. The women, children and babies would have to be taken into account before any attempt to stop them could be undertaken. Would the morning papers read:"Women and children gunned down by troopers"? The information indicated that many of the grownups would be armed, and it was unlikely that they would back down from a nose to nose confrontation. What if the road was blocked by trees and properly lit and all the officers withdrawn? No confrontation between the aggressors and the troopers could occur. Maybe then they would return to Canada, or go to another area in another jurisdiction, or try to enter the Moss lake area by way of the westerly side of the wilderness, using dirt roads to reach their target. But then, that could also be blocked in the same manner by patrols from the Lowville sub-station. One problem with this plan was that, with the Troopers withdrawn, the general public would be left with a hazardous situation (the trees) on the Big Moose Road, and how would the residents living beyond the roadblock travel? Perhaps the Indians were hell bent on a confrontation for publicity sake? What if they tried to take a hostage? "What if" became the question.

It was 7:30 p.m. when it occurred to him that there had been no orders from troop headquarters since he left the New Hartford Station over two hours before. Why so long? Did he misunderstand the captain's order? Was this a setup wherein he would have to make the final decision? After all, he was the officer on the scene and the acting zone commander. Was he going to be the fall guy if things went sour? He realized that Troop "D" Headquarters had to get orders from Division Headquarters after consultation with Governor Malcolm Wilson. Wilson no doubt would talk to the Federal Authorities for additional advice. Once decision making went to Division Headquarters it could take forever. They didn't have forever. Another twenty or thirty minutes, and it would be a moot point, as there would not be enough time to mobilize. Gallo actually toyed with the idea of doing his own thing, stopping the Indians and claiming that he received no radio message to the contrary. This was feasible as radio communications in that area of the mountains was practically non-existent. He reasoned that if he was successful the upper echelon would be thrilled, but if one Trooper or Indian was hurt, he would be charged with insubordination. He decided that following orders in this case would be the safe way (no injuries or death) and just dismissed the idea when it came. Deep in thought, he was startled when the Troop car radio squawked, "Call the Captain via phone."

"Do not intervene; let them enter," were the Captain's orders. A great sense of relief settled over him knowing that no one would die or be injured this night. The radio squawked again. This time it was the Troop "B" officer assigned to tail the Indians. He wanted to meet in the Hamlet of Inlet. The two officers met in the small town to discuss the matter further. The Investigator had a sheepish look on his face, stating, "I lost um when they came across the border." Apparently, the caravan split in all directions. All he was sure of was that they headed south into the State. Gallo was very upset and angered by this development. How could a seasoned Trooper lose fifty Indians in broad daylight?" After a short discussion with the officer about the orders to let them enter either location, Troop Headquarters was advised of the new development. Two troopers were brought in from the zone to monitor the arrival of the Mohawks. One was in position for Moss Lake, and the other for the Moose River Plains. It was after midnight when the Indian's cars and trucks began to filter into the Moss Lake Girls Camp. A cold soft rain began to fall over the area. What mattered most was that no one was going to die this night, but round one went to the Warrior Society as they entered their new home. They named it "Ganienkeh" the land of flint, pronounced in Mohawk (Gun-yung-gay).

After returning to the zone station, Gallo and Sergeant Martin discussed the evening's events. Martin would be in charge of the ensuing shift. The most intriguing item of the night was how certain people in the Old Forge area knew ahead of time that the Mohawks were coming. Another matter that bothered the Sergeants was that they knew the most precious possession of a Mohawk man was his women and children. Why then would they risk a bloody confrontation with women and children on board? The answer is simple; they wouldn't, not when their families were at risk. And how would the Indians know at the very last minute what the Troopers orders were concerning Moss Lake. All orders could change at the very last second. Yet, they somehow knew, that the danger to the women and children was minimal. How would they even know whether or not the Troopers were aware that the women and children were on board? Somehow, they knew the answers to all of these questions. The Mohawks had to leak the information of the takeover so that it would reach the State Police, and they had to be advised of last minute changes by an informant. Was there an informant close to the decision making process of the State Police, who could quickly advise the Mohawks of what action the Troopers would take? But, who in New York State was their agent? Was there a mole? There were however, other possibilities. The matter could be political and not within the State Police at all. Or, it could be someone within the Federal government. The possibilities were endless. Once again the thought about the Investigator losing the Indians lingered. It would not go away.

These thoughts created a dilemma. On the one hand, was it worth further follow up not knowing positively what had happened? Standard procedure would mandate the reporting of this to the Troop Commander. But, it was just a suspicion at this time, nothing more than that. On the other hand, if it was reduced to memorandum form, it would go through many hands. Too many members would be aware of its existence. The unknown agent might be inadvertently tipped off. If it was ignored and not reported, it might allow a mole to go undetected, the worst of all scenarios. Or, perhaps the blame might not lie within the State Police at all? The anxiety that they felt over what to do went away as soon as they settled on a plan. They decided to report the matter to the Zone Commander verbally, but they opted to wait until more thought could be put into the matter and to see if Chief Crofoot could uncover possible leads as to how the advanced information was obtained by the local businessmen. In the interim, perhaps something else would surface that would help to answer the question. At a later time the matter was discussed with the Troop Commander. But, that fact did not remove the matter from their minds. That strange event was securely embedded in their psyche, both men believing that this enigma would be answered in the near future.

This week, THE COURIER concludes its exclusive three-part story of the Moss Lake Indians takeover and occupation of state-owned land in the Central Adirondacks, near Big Moose and Eagle Bay. On May 13, 1978, the Indians will observe their fourth anniversary of the takeover. The concluding article begins on Page 8......

Pictured: Art Montour, one of the leaders and spokesman of the warrior society.

Chapter 4

A Moccasin In The Door

May 13, 1974, was a moccasin in the door for the Mohawks. They had stuck their foot in the Whiteman's door with great anticipation of the future. It had to be the most critical aspect of all their planning. However, little is known about their first night at Moss Lake except that, after the Indians tore down the State gate, they stretched their own cable across the entrance to the camp barring access to outsiders. From that time forward, they claimed sovereignty and forbade New York State to assert jurisdiction.

The Warriors maintained that the treaty of 1784 Fort Stanwick outlined the territory of the Mohawks, and the girls' camp was within that territory. The Whites had not conquered them in battle and therefore, they should not be held accountable to the White Man's law. Now all they had to do was to defend their repossession against action by the State to evict them, and explain to the local people and the press why they had taken over the State property.

The day following their arrival, they began distributing copies of the "Ganienkeh Manifesto" to the public and the media. This document outlined their plans to reestablish the Independent State of Ganienkeh on their ancient homeland and make the settlement a self-sufficient cooperative farming community. Many Whites of the area doubted the assertion that the Indians would make an attempt at agriculture at Moss Lake. There was not sufficient open land to cultivate and the soil was very acidic. The growing season was short, and nightly frosts, even in summer, were not conducive to producing crops.

The night of arrival at Moss Lake must have been very difficult for the Indians. Finding cover from the elements (cold mountain nights, rain and even snow) and battling the mosquitoes was a task not easily achieved, although there were many old buildings that would provide some shelter. Security had to be set up around the encampment to insure their safety from aggressors and/or wild animals (bear, coyotes and wolves). These animals were not normally a danger but the women and children feared them. The many unknowns that they were facing must have driven their anxiety level very high, not knowing what to expect next. Would the Troopers attack in the morning? Were they already there hiding somewhere in the forest? Would the remainder of the Warriors Society and their wives and children find the encampment without further trouble? But, all went well for the Indians that night and sun up must have brought great relief. `

The following morning the Warriors erected a large Ganienkeh sign:

THIS AREA IS PART OF THE LAND UNDER THE LEGAL AND ABORIGINAL TITLE OF THE MOHAWK NATION. WE MOHAWKS HAVE RETURNED TO OUR HOMELAND, WITH THE HELP OF OTHER TRADITIONAL INDIANS WHO WISH TO LIVE ACCORDING TO THEIR OWN CULTURE, CUSTOMS AND TRADITION. NATIVE NATIONS ALL OVER THE WORLD HAVE REGAINED THEIR LANDS. U.S. RESTORED OKINOWA TO JAPAN. WE ASSUME THAT THE RENDERING OF JUSTICE SHALL BE EXTENDED TO THE AMERICAN INDIANS AND THIS LAND SHALL BE RESTORED TO THE MOHAWKS. THE CAMP IS OUT TO PROVE THAT TRADITIONAL INDIANS CAN LIVE OFF THE LAND WITHOUT ELECTRICITY, MONEY, WELFARE RELIEF OR AID OF ANY KIND. WHITE PEOPLE ARE ASKED TO HELP BY NOT ENTERFERING, ALL WE NEED IS TO BE LEFT ALONE AND LIVE OUR OWN WAY.

That day, the Indians also erected a large tee pee across the roadway from the entrance gate to Moss Lake, so as to be visible for the public and the press. From there they distributed the manifesto. Some locals actually helped with the distribution of the Indian brochures, but, no one was allowed beyond the gate at the entrance. And, no one was allowed to take pictures, even the press. The Indians would orchestrate any and all photo-ops. The press obtained some of these pictures and printed them in the local papers. The locals began to realize that they had some encroachers in their neck of the woods and to wonder, what were they really after.

Ranger Bill Marleau of Big Moose arrived at the gate in the afternoon of that first day and advised the Mohawks that they were trespassing. The Indians said, "You are the trespasser," and refused to allow him through the gate. After several tries to evict the Indians, the ranger called his superiors in Albany and was advised to "Leave the Indians alone." The following day they erected another sign. It said, "Ganienkeh," with an eagle below and the words "Six Nation Iroquois Confederacy, Mohawk Eastern door of the Long House." (Report to COPCA by Blair)

The actual number of Mohawks was unknown, but as time went on, it was speculated that approximately thirty men, women and children arrived that first night, more arriving in the next few days. This number grew when the comfort zone of the Indians increased and more felt reassured that the State Police would not attack. The Mohawks appointed one of their most competent Warriors to head up their security Earl Cross, and it improved almost daily. State politicians openly stated that there would be no effort to dislodge the Mohawks by force. As time wore on, it was further estimated, that as many as one hundred full-time traditionals were at the camp. Complacency wasn't in their playbook, and they continued to improve their security as time would permit. This reassured the people within of their safety.

The State's failure to show some sign of strength to dislodge the encroachers resulted in the Warrior leaders becoming bolder and growing horns. On May 20, 1974, over one hundred local residents crowded into the front of the Ganienkeh gate to listen to a public hearing set up by the Mohawks. Most of the listeners were in total shock as they listened to the Indians advise them that Ganienkeh was just the start of a new North American Indian State. And then the real shocker: They were claiming most of upper New York State and all of the State of Vermont, which was comprised of nine million acres. It was made clear that they would accept nothing less and would fight for the repossession of this land, which they declared had been stolen from them by the White Man. Many Whites thought that it was perhaps a joke, but it was not. The Warrior Society was dead serious, and when the meeting was over, most realized that the Indian declaration was for real. Things had become very critical in the Central Adirondacks of New York State.

The activities within the encampment, and any new items of interest, were brought to the attention of State Police daily, describing how the camp was protected. Included within this information were the details regarding the identities of the people inside the Moss Lake Impoundment? The Troopers joked amongst themselves that they knew what the Mohawks were having for breakfast and what was on the menu for tomorrow's lunch from the intelligence they were receiving. The indispensable information, the Mohawk's security preparations and occupants, mostly came from other Indian reservations and/or territories in the United States and Canada. What was happening at Moss Lake was of great interest to all Indians in North America. The security package was the major concern of the troopers who had to plan for a possible assault on the Mohawks in an effort to regain the State property. Chief Louis Hall (Karoniaktajeh) made absolutely sure that the quiver at Moss Lake was always full. He took nothing for granted. Along with other security matters, the Troopers were most interested in the identity of the occupants and cache of weapons said to be within the stronghold. Senior Investigator Richard Gildersleeve of the State Police kept close tabs on all important information with regard to the Indian occupation, keeping the Zone office and Major Charland informed.

In addition to the police, the Warriors also had to worry about the general public traveling the Big Moose Road and/or walking the trails in the State Forest surrounding the 612 acre girls' camp. Trees were cut and used to build the two log bunkers on the Big Moose Road, each constantly manned by two braves with fully automatic weapons. The Troopers learned that the warriors constructed an additional bunker at the rear of the lake, likewise attended by security guards. Indian Scouts that walked the trails carrying weapons challenged any person or persons in the area and escorted them out of their territory. Many encounters of this kind occurred at the perimeter of the encampment, within the heavily forested area according to informants. One such incident took place on the Bubb Lake trail. During hunting season, two Whites were walking the trail with weapons in hand, when several Indian scouts confronted them. After being told to leave the area, an argument ensued concerning the rights of the Whites and that of the Indians. They could see more warriors behind the trees in the shadows, and the man stated to his wife, "Take off your safe," making her ready for any eventuality. The Indian scouts did not yield and the man and woman, fearing for their lives, left without further incident.

Another problem for the Mohawks and State Police was the upcoming snowmobile and hunting season and the many trails that went through their new territory that led from Old Forge, Inlet and Eagle Bay to the Big Moose area. It wasn't long before the chainsaws of the Long House people were buzzing, knocking down trees, felling them across the snowmobile trails to block the general public and/or the troopers. Eventually, the trails were posted by the Mohawks. Their signs read: "Repossessed GANIENKEH (Mohawk) TERRITORY - patrolled by the Warrior Society - No Trespassing." The Warriors did not discriminate. Many White's and Black's who inadvertently found themselves in the Ganienkeh area were escorted from the territory at gunpoint by the Warriors. If Indians not associated with the encampment were found, they most likely would have been escorted out as well. It became very apparent that the Warrior Society was deeply embedded in the land that they had repossessed. But, it also started to rub heavily on the local people who were becoming impatient with the State's inaction, and the growing boldness of the Warrior Society. Who could blame them!

Local people of the area stand in total disbelief

Indian occupation

Chapter 5

Tears In His Voice

The Mohawks arrived at the Moss Lake encampment with practically nothing to sustain their existence. They only had a few staples, clothing and weapons they could hunt and/or defend their repossessed territory with. At first, they stated that they wanted no help from the Whites of the area that the Whites could help by just leaving them alone. However, as their needs continued to grow, they changed their policy and began to appeal to the church groups of the State and other charities available. A plan to win over the press was almost immediately put into action, starting with the posting and publishing of the Ganienkeh Manifesto, which included handing out brochures to the public. The media was preoccupied with Watergate and President Nixon and gave little attention to the Moss Lake incursion. The Warriors had a much more powerful weapon in the wings that they put into action to reach the hearts of the people and to help to gain the media's attention.

Arthur Montour (Kakwirakeron) was that weapon. He had been designated as the official spokesman of the Mohawks by the traditional people. He was a very low key and humble appearing Indian male in his late twenties, about six feet tall with a slender muscular build. He was quite handsome and appealed to his audiences in many ways including his obvious leadership qualities. He was exactly what the doctor had ordered for a representative of the Indians and the press loved him. He would appear before them and other audiences in full traditional Mohawk attire, wearing buckskin shirts with white beads hanging down from around his neck. His hair was dark brown and displayed in long braids hanging almost halfway down to his waist. Montour was a picture of what the public expected a Mohawk Warrior to look like. His English was very good and to say he was mild mannered would be an understatement. But, what mattered most about his attributes, was his ability to rope in those that listened to him. He did this through reciting the Mohawk's plight through history and with the uncanny way he could put tears in his voice, grabbing his listeners' inner feelings for oppressed, downtrodden minorities, and, oh boy, did it ever work! The press for the most part became pro Indian and their favorable coverage put additional pressure on the State politicians to negotiate with the Mohawks.

Montour spoke at practically every campus in the State. He appeared on television and radio talk shows and debated the issues of how the Indians were attempting to return to the old ways of living and why their repossession of land was in their eyes proper and correct. He always made note of the fact that the land they were after, nine million acres of upper New York State and Vermont, was mostly public land. And they, the Mohawks, did not wish to usurp private land of the White's. He started each public speaking engagement with an Indian prayer and then interpreted it in English.

A significant part of Montour's presentation would include the historical saga of the "Wampum Belt." The Traditionalists' believed that the White Man and the Indian should travel different routes through life and should be kept separate but parallel to one another. This they said was told by the "Wampum Belt" which was made up of two rows of purple beads set out on a white background and tied together with buckskin lace. One row was the White Man's route and the second row the Mohawk (traditionalist) route through life. Early on, the American Indian used Quahog shells (Clam Shells) to tell his story on the wampum belt. In time, sophisticated beads replaced the clam shells. The saga of the Wampum belt, it was said, was first started when the Dutch settlers to the area entered into a treaty with the Mohawks.

Another symbol of this belief was that of two separate vessels traveling down a river, one a canoe for the Indians and the other a boat or ship for the White man. The symbols advocate that neither group should step into the other's vessel, lest one or both should capsize. Further, if one should try to keep one foot in each boat and straddle the water, a wave could cause that person to fall in. If one or the other stepped into the other's boat or canoe, and it did not capsize, then they were there to stay. In other words, the Traditional Indian should lead his life as he did in the distant past, without the conveniences and commercialism of the materialistic White Man.

A local White man, believed to be Arthur Einhorn, a professor of anthropology at Jefferson Community College in Watertown, who made replicas of Indian artifacts, agreed to make a wampum belt for the Mohawks. He had spoken at length with Montour at the camp's gate, gaining understanding between the two. Most believed that Einhorn was very much on the side of the Indians' takeover of the Moss Lake Girl's Camp and was known as an avid collector of Indian lore and artifacts. Upon its completion, the belt was presented to Montour by the man's son. The belt's background was white beads with two horizontal lines of purple beads obtained from Czechoslovakia. Strips of rawhide held the beads in place, and had been dyed with black walnut bark. The belt was encased in a green bag and could be closed from the top with a rawhide drawstring. At the end of the rawhide drawstring, were two red Catholic rosary beads. From that day forward, Montour included the wampum belt story in many of his appearances and presented the belt to his audiences, but never presented it as authentic. It became a very popular symbol for discussion and would create much interest. The story and display of the belt proved to be a masterful way to capture the participation of those present. Montour almost always carried the belt with him.

Michael Blair, the spokesman for COPCA, in a report to them, believed parts of the belt (Rosary beads) were included as a joke and because of that, it was not a true replica of a Wampum Belt. Of course, the Mohawks did not profess the Catholic faith and Blair felt this was a slap in the face to the Indians. It was presented to Montour by its maker in good faith, and, it is not believed that Einhorn meant anything other than a friendly gesture between the two men. What is positively known is that the Indians got a whole lot of mileage from its possession. At that time of the insurrection, the Warriors paid little attention to what faith they were receiving their bread and butter from and the Catholic beads did not offend them.

Even though it was known that the Warrior Society denounced the Christian faith, churches from all over the State and other Christian groups gave to fulfill the Indians needs. Some offered food and supplies and others gave in cash. This speaks well for the organizations that found it necessary to help their fellow man. The Indian's faith and beliefs had nothing to do with it at all. Church groups throughout the area seemed to be the greatest contributors, starting almost immediately upon the Mohawk's arrival.

In March of 1975, the Corning Leader newspaper of Corning, New York published a very controversial article, requesting aid for the Mohawk people at Moss Lake. Its' Chairman, Robert Gill, had recently visited the encampment at the request of Montour. He stated, "The people at Eagle Bay are literally starving." He asked the residents of the area for canned and bulk foods and for shovels, rakes and spades, including, of course, seeds and seed potatoes. Also required for their gardening program were plows and cultivating equipment. In addition to those items, the Indians needed buckets for collecting the sap from hard maple trees. The Indians had already procured the evaporating mechanism needed for the manufacture of Maple Syrup, as the sap gathering season was about to begin. Hay and grain for the cattle at Moss Lake were also included in the request.

Gill stated that calls coming in were thirty five to one in favor of the humanitarian drive he had started. For those that did not agree, Gill wrote in the newspaper, "I know they are hungry. I have seen this with my own eyes. That's my concern, to get food to people who are hungry. I may agree or disagree with their philosophy, but that is my concern."

On March 24, 1975 at about 2:00 p.m., a large yellow truck passed the first Trooper outpost and traveled slowly up the poorly maintained road, pulling into the front gate of Ganienkeh. In moments, men, women, children and many local volunteers formed a human chain to unload the heavily laden vehicle. These materials from Gill's efforts were carried to and stored in the few buildings closest to the gate. It appeared that along with others throughout the State, Montour and Gill did what many thought would be impossible.

On the negative side, an employee of the Town of Webb Sanitation Department, who wished to remain anonymous stated, "My job was to push the garbage over the side at the dump! Many times I pushed boxes of good food over the edge that had been dropped there by the Indians. Once they had money they would buy what they wanted."

After the sap gathering season, and the making of maple syrup, the Mohawks boasted that they had made hundreds of gallons of syrup. The local White community laughed at their declaration, knowing that only a few hard maple trees existed in the Moss Lake area.

Some of the local whites of the township accused the Indians of purchasing their "hush supplies" out of town. Meaning, lobsters, shrimp, steaks, (the big money items) and the various types of libation

As a result of the work of Art Montour and the other Mohawk spokespersons, some large amounts of money were obtained from different organizations. On June 25, 1975 the Presbyterian Church's National Self Development Committee pledged $26,000 to the Mohawks' in spite of the local church giving advice to the contrary. The money, which was to purchase two trucks and a tractor with plow and harrow and twenty head of buffalo, had already been partially given to the Indians in the amount of $13,000. Before hand, in January, the Ganienkeh Indians had applied for $5,000 to help establish a farming community. They went directly to the National Self-Development Committee instead of the local church in Utica. In a letter, the local presbytery warned the National Self Development Committee that this was a hopeless endeavor because the land at Ganienkeh was not conducive to agriculture, and the project did not fall within the guidelines of the organization. The committee ignored their advice and awarded the money. The Indians purchased a tractor and a truck, and at a later date, received the additional $13,000. The grazing land at Ganienkeh was non-existent. This indicated that the Indians intended to pasture the buffalo at the new Ganienkeh, yet to be established. The Mohawks continued every effort to raise money and do it in even a small amounts.

One quiet summer evening while Montour was out raising money for the people of Ganienkeh, he walked into the State Police Station in New Hartford, and in his usual calm manner, asked to talk to whoever was in charge. He explained to Zone Sergeant Gallo that he had picked up $425.00 in cash for speaking at a church mass in Clinton, New York. He had put the money in a brown paper bag to take back to Ganienkeh. He stopped first at the Warehouse Food Market on Route 12B in Clinton to purchase groceries. He removed money for the groceries from the bag and when he returned from the market, he placed the remainder back into the brown paper container, but inadvertently left the sack of money on the roof of his car and drove off. He had traveled over a mile before he realized what he had done. A detail of five troopers walked both sides of the roadway from the market to the point where he discovered the money missing, (but with negative results.) Montour seemed surprised that the Troopers would help him and expressed his thanks many times over during the search. A teletype message was sent to police agencies of New York State regarding the missing money, however the cash was never recovered.

Even though individual Indians continued to pursue financial help on their own, white support groups such as RAIN (Rights For American Indians Now) opened chapters in cities throughout New York State, while other White support groups publicized Ganienkeh, organizing financial, legal and political aid. The Mohawk's were now in the National and International spotlight and the media loved it, and so did the Indians. Art Montour could take a bow for what he had accomplished as spokesman and one of the leaders of the Mohawk's.

Over time, different organizations and agencies aligned themselves as either "Pro" or "Con" with regard to the Indians. Many who were on the fence, were brought over to the Indian side by the work of Montour and his aides. Anthropologist Arthur Einhorn of Jefferson County Community College in Watertown, New York, saw the division as follows:

"PRO GANIENKEH"

1. AIM (American Indian Movement) of the U.S., Canada and Hamburg Germany
2. North American Indian Club of Syracuse
3. Six Nations council
4. Reservation Indian Leadership
5. Traditionalists of Caughnawaga Reservation
6. Traditionalists of Saint Regis Reservation

7. White citizens groups - RAIN,
8. Legal organizations
9. Churches (eighteen in all)
10. Indian awareness groups
11. News media - WOTT radio, WWNY TV, Watertown Daily Times.
12. Catholic Press
13. Akwesasne Notes

"CON GANIENKEH"

1. Government and State Agencies - Attorney General,
2. State Police
3. Supreme Court
4. Adirondack Park Association
5. Local Senators and Assemblymen
6. District Attorney
7. Federal government and agencies
8. Vice President's Domestic Counsel
9. Alcohol and Tobacco and Firearms (ATF)
10. Reservation Indian Leadership
11. Caughnawaga Council
12. Saint Regis Council
13. COPCA - white citizen groups
14. F.B.I.

The "pro" Ganienkeh groups shown above were not all "pro" Ganienkeh from the very beginning, but the result of the Indians' public relations campaign. The Mohawks seemed to have all of their ducks in a row in a well thought out plan to win over as much support as possible. Of course, the tears in Montour's voice lassoed any individuals already on the fence, providing that little push that was needed, particularly those that were liberal in nature and subject to minority appeal. The people of the State were giving to the Indians like candy to trick-or-treaters at Halloween.

Louis Hall (Karoniaktejeh), Royener and Secretary of Ganienkeh

Chapter 6

Indian Summer

The summer of 1974 was anything but a traditional summer in the northern Adirondacks. The locals, the Indians, the State Police, the Town of Webb Police, DEC officers and, of course, the State of New York, were all preoccupied with the events that were unfolding each day. It made for great gossip over a hot cup of coffee or a cold beer. The Moss Lake affair gave people something of interest to talk about, and, almost daily, the papers would have an interesting story about the Mohawk incursion. Although it was stressful for everyone, it was a somewhat happy and flourishing time for the Mohawks.

Many of the local people in the Township initially believed that the Mohawk's arrival would help the economy, including Bob Hall, the Director of Tourism. It would be only a short time before the State made a move to evict the trespassers. The businessmen of the area believed that when the tourists heard of the Indian repossession of the Moss Lake Girls' Camp it would romanticize the North woods in their minds. There would be Indians in full head dress and native apparel wielding tomahawks. Braves wearing only loin cloths to cover their privates and war paint on their faces would be everywhere. War whoops and dancing around the counsel fires to the constant beat of a distant drum would be the norm. This, the locals believed, would certainly glamorize the mountains of the Adirondack Park, and put the area on the map. These optimists could see a fruitful tourist season ahead and the dollars rolling in.

But, no doubt, to their disappointment, the encampment was closed to all outsiders and remained a mystery. No one could get past the guarded gate staffed by two sentries. What were they hiding? What didn't they want the outside world to see? Perhaps this posture also worked to increase the intrigue of the Indian encampment. Even other Indians, if not traditional, were not allowed admittance. After Christmas, a warrior who was not Christian took his young son from Ganienkeh to Akwesasne to visit his grandmother. The Indians at Akwesasne were Christian and celebrated Christmas. The grandmother asked her grandson what he got for Christmas from Santa Claus. He replied, "Nothing, they wouldn't let him through the gate." (Sovereignty and Symbol - Landsman 1988)

When those inside made an outside appearance, their dress was pretty much the same as the White Man of the area. Only those who were authorized Mohawk spokespersons, when in public, dressed in a somewhat traditional Indian manner, particularly when interviewed by the press, or making a speaking engagement. At times, just a feather in their hair would be the only clue identifying an Indian from a White. Their skin was sometimes as white as the locals, which made it harder to detect if they were white or red. Some of the Mohawks exhibited slightly olive and/or sun tanned skin. Arthur Montour (Kakwirakeron), the main spokesman for the group, almost always appeared in full Mohawk dress. His skin was closer to that of a white than an Indian.

Although the summer was quite tranquil for the Redman, there were those Whites in the area that were angry about the takeover from the very beginning. They cited the State's hands off policy, the double standard of the rule of law, and the fact that most of the Mohawks were Canadian, as the basis for their anger. Yet, they were powerless to do anything about it. They wondered if the State was aware of the Indian action before hand and if so, why were they, (the Indians), allowed to take over the Girls' Camp with impunity. Police Officers of the area, including State Troopers, also disliked the double standard of justice which tied their hands. They knew that their enforcement in the area with regard to the White's had to be very carefully thought out before any action could be taken. As time passed, and the issue continued to fester, and be ignored by State and Federal Governments, the anger of the locals grew intense. This no doubt, was one of the catalysts that led to future formation of the area Vigilantes. This anger did not affect the Mohawks attempt at carrying on a somewhat mediocre attempt at farming.

During the early spring and summer, the aborigines not only fortified their stronghold, but began moving in farm animals: horses, cows, chickens, pigs, ducks and geese. The animals running loose agitated the locals who had to drive with extra caution on the Big Moose Road. On one summer day, a newsman from Boonville, New York accidently ran over a chicken and claimed to have been chased by the Indians. That same summer, Betty Barnum of Big Moose, was traveling past the encampment going towards Eagle Bay when she also ran over a chicken. She was so afraid of the Mohawks that she didn't stop until she got to Eagle Bay. She spent two hours just sitting in her car afraid to travel back through Ganienkeh to Big Moose. She believed that the Indians would sprinkle corn on and across the road so the chickens would get hit and the Mohawks could then start an incident. After settling her nerves, she drove back to Big Moose, suffering much anxiety on the way. Betty's incident with the chicken is an example of the fears that the people of Big Moose had to endure every day of the week, and the reason they had to walk softly in their every day routines.

The cattle grazed their way on the shoulders of the roadway each day until they reached Eagle Bay, then onto the lawns of the homes next to the road. Many times they were chased from the grounds of Camp Gorham (a YMCA boy's camp located almost next to Moss Lake) only to return the following day. Complaints were lodged with the State Police, who, in turn, contacted the Indians in an effort to solve the problem. That effort was like spitting in the wind. There was hardly any grazing land at Moss Lake and the Indians did not have the money to buy hay.

On one such day, a full grown milking cow wandered onto the lawn of a local man who had made several previous complaints concerning the animal. Out of anger, he picked up his rifle and shot the animal. When troopers arrived, they found the cow lying dead on the shooters lawn, surrounded by several Indian males. Zone Sergeant Gallo was asked to respond to the scene by the Troopers. He traveled from the Zone Station in New Hartford to Eagle Bay and spent several precarious moments defusing the situation. Gallo was presented with conflicting emotions: On the one hand, he detested people who take out their aggressions on innocent animals, and, in any other situation, he would have ordered the Troopers to arrest the man for cruelty to animals. On the other hand, he knew that an arrest of a local White Man would be the "coup de grace" for a major escalation of the conflict. The Mohawks solved his dilemma by refusing to prosecute the shooter. Gallo was very curt to the shooter, attempting to send a strong message, "Why the cow? And why do you want to start another serious point of aggravation between the two parties?" He had to bite his tongue as most officers have to do from time to time when they should not express an opinion. The Indians summoned a tow truck from nearby Eagle Bay and towed the cow back to the Moss Lake Encampment, where they no doubt utilized it as beef. The Mohawks did not make an issue of the event and it went unnoticed by the media. Knowing that winter was on its way, three Indian males went to work on a farm in Boonville, not for cash, but for hay for their cattle. This showed an effort by the Mohawks to solve their problem with wandering cattle and to relieve some of the tensions of the community. But, those feelings were not gone, and only grew more intense with the inaction of the government.

The State did not move against the Indians as most had hoped for and seemed to ignore their presence. The lame duck Governor, Malcolm Wilson, through his spokesperson, pretended to make little of the situation, and, again, let it be known that the State did not intend to take action against the Indians. Through a press release, the DEC indicated that they would take no precipitous action, but felt that the Indian land claim was without merit. (Troy Record 4/25/75) The locals were no longer sitting on the fence with regard to the Indians, and became anxious and angry, hoping for, and demanding, the removal of the trespassers. Additionally, they were not being advised by the State of matters pertaining to the Mohawks and were being left in the dark. It was as though they, the locals, were a non-entity.

After much prodding by the locals and their politicians, the State finally took some "save face" action. In September of 1974, the DEC requested that the State bring the Mohawk's claim to the U.S. District court of Judge Port (N.Y. vs. Danny White et al. 74 civ 370 N.D.N.Y.1974). The intent of the lawsuit was to clarify once and for all that the State was the lawful owner of the nine million acres of upper New York State and Vermont and to validate the 1797 Joseph Brandt Treaty that would show that the six nations had legally sold the land in question to New York State. The case would not be heard until early 1975 and was for the time being adjourned.

During that first summer at Moss Lake, many other events of interest took place, such as small conflicts between the parties and the Mohawks claims of constant harassment from the Whites. The atmosphere was notably changing and things were about to take a turn for the worst as fall approached. A cold wind was blowing in the Central Adirondack Mountains.

Chapter 7

The Young Vigilantes

In 1892, the Adirondack Park was established in northern New York State and marked out by what has been known as the Blue Line. The park is a vast wilderness with nearly 6 million acres of timberland and pristine lakes. In 1972, the downstate politicians, representing such interests as New York City, fought a ferocious battle in the State legislature with upstate politicians in an effort to create the Adirondack Park Agency (APA). The downstate interests won out and control of the Adirondack Park went to the city folks, which included the "Big Brother Law," much to the chagrin of politicians and residents within the park. Although it was called the Master Plan, it really was the zoning laws (The Big Brother Law) that were passed by the State legislature that now controlled this vast area of the Adirondacks.

In 1973, the locals were further infuriated when these land use rules came into effect, which really was the purpose of the "Big Brother Law" in the first place. They now realized how restrictive these rules would be. The Adirondack Park Agency was born to govern how the residents would use their land (construction, development, commercial use, etc.) without any input from the people affected. The Big Brother Law was much more restrictive than normal zoning, resulting in the government's never-ending involvement in the affairs of the local people, and many of the restrictions stood in conflict with the U.S. Constitution. No effort was made to install local representation. The agency was made part of the Department of Environmental Conservation (DEC) with offices in Raybrook, New York, just to the west of Lake Placid.

The locals saw this as downstate ruling the ignorant upstaters for their own good, but really for downstate interests. Newspaper articles began appearing chastising the agency and its employees for overzealous enforcement of the rules. Being a form of a policing agency, the agents failed to establish a rapport with the locals and wouldn't cooperate with local requests for leniency. Many editorials were written blasting the agency. The APA had designated certain areas as forever wild and disallowed aircraft to use the seventeen lakes and ponds therein. The locals attempted to get the agency to reverse its ruling, citing the need for aircraft to use these spots to ferry hunters, fishermen, hikers and campers in and out. They pointed out how the local economies were dependent on these activities to survive. The APA refused to back down and the owners of the airplanes lost half of their business. Some even went out of business entirely. Anger continued to mount within the park and there was one report of a State Police Sergeant refusing to assist the agency with a particularly difficult action that had to be completed. The reputation of the APA was one of a Gestapo-like police force.

On November 11, 1973, an article appeared in the Albany Times concerning the feelings of Environmental Commissioner Ogden Reid: "Recent tactics by the Adirondack Park Agency have displeased Environmental Commissioner Ogden Reid, who thinks the agencies staffers have been too heavy handed in their zealous enforcement of park regulations." It became apparent that the APA would have to lighten up, or the agency's future would be in jeopardy. A lesson learned, the agency began to moderate its' tactics and enforcement, particularly with the addition of local boards to work with the hated State Agency.

When the Warrior Society arrived in Moss Lake, the local people were already alienated from the State as a result of the APA. Then the Department of Environmental Conservation Commissioner, Ogden Reed, made the announcement that, although he did not condone the action of the Mohawk's, no action would be taken to dislodge them. In view of the State's hands-off policy, the local people began to see it for what it was: a double standard of justice. It became a sore thumb and the talk of the mountains. When the locals learned of more catering to the whims of the Indians and preventing the State Police from enforcing the law with regard to the Mohawks, their anger reached new plateaus on the Richter scale. Unfortunately, they vented their anger verbally on anyone that would listen regarding the Indians whom they now considered renegades.

As the issue festered and the local teenagers listened and saw the frustration in their parents and their inability to do anything about the situation, they decided that they should take some action. They formed small groups of five or six boys and late at night went off on their missions. At first, they would just whoop and holler and mock the Indians as they drove past the encampment, throwing firecrackers from the windows of their cars. However, as they became more daring, their activities escalated. One night they drove circles around the Tee Pee standing at the front gate, throwing gravel and dirt into the air while enduring gunfire from the encampment, which probably went harmlessly in the air, meant to scare the vigilantes. Luckily, no one was injured during this daring maneuver. Shortly thereafter, the Teepee disappeared. The Iroquois had lived in long houses made of birch bark, that being how they obtained the name "Long House People." Only the Indians of the western plains lived in teepees. But, it is believed that the Mohawks were aware of the difference and simply had used the teepee as a symbol of the American Indians presence.

Perhaps, the most daring of all of the vigilantes ventures, was the late night theft of the Ganienkeh flag. The Indians never reported this theft to the State Police, probably because of the embarrassment involved. As souvenirs, the boys cut the flag into five pieces, each perpetrator keeping a section. For unknown reasons, the informant concerning the theft of the flag would not provide details of the daring venture, but was able to produce his share of the flag as proof. He also would not reveal the names of the other youths involved in the daring acts of harassment. Throughout these missions, the young vigilantes could not have realized the serious consequences of what they were doing and what these acts would eventually lead to.

One of the youngsters believing that he needed a firearm as protection obtained an old shotgun. In an effort to keep it concealed, he cut off the barrel to make the weapon shorter and easier to hide. He also wanted to keep it legal should it be discovered by the police. He learned that the barrel had to be one quarter inch more than eighteen inches, so he measured and cut the barrel with his hacksaw. A few days later, when stopped by the State Police, the trooper spotted the weapon on the floor of the car. The young vigilante discovered he had made a costly mistake. He measured incorrectly and had cut the barrel a quarter inch shorter then eighteen inches instead of a quarter inch longer. He was arrested for possession of a dangerous weapon.

Other vigilante groups formed in the area and were conducting similar acts of harassment against the Indians. These acts, no doubt, helped lead to the eventual shooting of Stephen Drake and Aprile Madigan. When this tragedy occurred the young vigilantes took a respite out of fear. They did not want to get shot, but it didn't stop their planning. The next planned move was to sneak into the backside of Moss Lake on a moonless night by way of the Bubb Lake Trail, swimming two hundred plus yards to the island in the center of the lake. This was a very dangerous move in the cold waters of an Adirondack lake in the fall or winter. They believed that the Mohawks, upon awakening, would see them there and call the State Police to remove them. The vigilantes saw this as a way to get the Troopers inside the gate of Ganienkeh and perhaps instigate an altercation between the Mohawks and the State Police and lead to the eviction by force of the Indians. Fortunately, the plan was never carried out, possibly having been stopped by Trooper Bill Chesebro after he learned of its existence. Chesebro would leak the word that the Troopers had now identified all of the vigilantes. This worried the youngsters that their arrest may be imminent.

At the time of the Indian occupation of the Moss Lake Camp, the State Police were aware of the Vigilante groups operating and had identified some of them, but they were without proof to prosecute them as juvenile delinquents or young adults. Trooper Bill Chesebro made contact with the suspected youths on several occasions, warning them of the consequences of their acts. The troopers also believed that local adults were infiltrating the camp at night and causing chaos. Several reports of this nature came from the Indians throughout their occupation of the Girls' Camp. The phantom vigilantes would enter the encampment during the early morning hours when the moon was not in the sky and rattle doors and windows, making the Indians believe they were trying to break into the buildings. This, no doubt, terrified the

Mohawks. They had no way of knowing what the intruder or intruders' intent really was. There was much speculation in the area as to who the perpetrators were. Some even believed that law enforcement was behind the harassment. The theory was that the officers were frustrated and angry with their tied hands and needed a way to vent their inhibitions. No evidence ever surfaced that would indicate police involvement. As a matter of fact, no evidence ever surfaced that these reports were authentic. The occupant's complaints could not be verified or proper on site investigations conducted without interviews and entry to the camp. Police action was thwarted by the Mohawks as they continued to insist that the State had no jurisdiction on the Nation of Ganienkeh. However, this did not stop them from logging the complaints with the troopers, no doubt to use in future negotiations with the State and Federal governments, and to gain sympathy of the remainder of State occupants.

*State Negotiator Ogden Reid, unknown subject,
Robert Wurz, and Doug Bennett*

*Pictured: Wayne Martin as First Sergeant,
a promotion later on in his career.*

Drake brothers as they appear today

Home again

Aprile Ann Madigan plays with "Snoopy" while "Chocolate" ignores them both. (Times photo by Stella Cecere)

Chapter 8

Circle The Wagons

For several weeks, the honking of Canada Geese could be heard as they beat their wings heading for warmer parts, forecasting that snow was soon to come to the North Country. The autumn leaves had fallen from the hard and soft maples and from the beach and birch, taking away the beautiful colors of autumn: red, orange, yellow and purple, leaving a grey hue to the landscape. The evergreens (balsam, spruce and hemlock) provided the north woods with a sprinkling of green, and the forest floor was now covered with the autumn leaves, giving off one of nature's most perfect scents.

It was Monday, October 28, 1974, the third day of deer hunting season in the northern tier of New York State. Over the past weekend the clocks had been turned back and darkness would set in around 5:00 p.m... It was approximately 5:15 p.m. and already dark when the Drake brothers, Stephen and Michael, left a local watering hole in Eagle Bay to drive to Big Moose to pick up a friend for a night out. As they passed the Moss Lake Indian encampment, the Drake's hollered and war whooped at the Warriors in their usual manner. This sort of harassment was nothing new. The youths of the area, when traveling past the Indian stronghold, would almost always whoop and holler. This time their harassment was met with gunfire from Ganienkeh, three rifle shots ringing out. What the Drakes didn't know was that the Indian leaders (elders) were not present at the encampment; they had left for a meeting elsewhere, and the young braves were easily taunted into action. The Drakes sped off to Big Moose where they found the

Big Moose Inn closed. The boys managed to awaken Doug and Bonnie Bennett, the proprietors, by pounding on the door. It was the Bennett's day off and they were taking an afternoon nap. After much persuasion from Doug Bennett, the Drakes used the phone and called State Police, to lodge their complaint.

Trooper John Schreck received the call from Stephen Drake. Drake believed Schreck told him that Trooper Smith would be dispatched directly to the area of the shooting at Ganienkeh. Schreck immediately contacted Trooper Al Smith of State Police, Old Forge, via radio, advising him of the complaint. Smith acknowledged receipt of the transmission with his shield number but somehow failed to respond to the area of the shooting. It was later learned, that instead of responding to Ganienkeh, the Trooper went to the Drake's Inn, in Inlet, owned by the father of the Drake boys, expecting to meet the complainant there. There is little doubt that the transmission he received from Schreck was garbled; as many radio signals are in this region of the mountains. Had Trooper Smith understood Trooper Schreck's transmission completely, the eventual shooting incidents may have been avoided. Radio transmissions were recorded at Troop Headquarters, but only kept for a short period of time before they were erased, and no one recognized the importance of this radio transmission until it was too late.

After approximately a thirty minute wait at the Big Moose Inn, the Drakes believed the Troopers would be at the Indian encampment and their trip back through Ganienkeh would be safe. The brothers then headed back towards Eagle Bay at approximately 6:00 p.m. right into the jaws of the dragon. As they reached the flat stretch of the Big Moose Road in front of Ganienkeh, Stephen stopped the car. They were shocked to see the roadway lined with warriors carrying various weapons. The young braves were waiting and knew the Drake car, which they had seen many times before. The Drakes were in the cross-hairs of fully automatic rifles (AK-14's), shotguns loaded with double-0 buckshot, and 30 caliber deer rifles. When Stephen Drake was later asked how many braves were on the edge of the Big Moose Road that evening, his answer was, "There could have been ten or maybe twenty. All I know for sure is that there were a whole lot of Indians." Stephen, who was driving, crouched down towards the center of the car with only his left hand on the wheel. He floored the accelerator and ran the gauntlet of Indian marksmen. Their car was riddled with bullets, one striking and penetrating Stephen's left shoulder. The back window was blown out and two bullets were imbedded in the dashboard. Holes made by buckshot were all over the vehicle. Based on the appearance of the car, it was remarkable that they were not killed by the amount of projectiles that penetrated the auto. Stephen believed that the .35 caliber armor piercing round that struck him in the shoulder was fired by a brave in a tree. The angle of entry through the windshield, and his position (low and in the center of the front seat when struck) indicate that he was correct in his belief. The Indians stated afterwards that the Drakes had both times fired first as they drove by the Mohawk encampment, and this was why, they, the Indians returned fire.

The Drake brothers drove as fast as they could away from the Indians. Stephen, who was bleeding profusely and on the verge of shock, managed to stop the car. Michael dragged his brother from beneath the wheel to the passenger side of the vehicle and commenced driving on the narrow bumpy road. The car shuttered to a stop at the home of Conservation officer George Sehring. The Chrysler convertible had two flat tires and gasoline was pouring from the tank. Nancy Sehring grabbed two Kotex pads and applied them to each side of Stephen's shoulder, trying to stop the gushing flow of blood, while George called the Inlet Ambulance, which was the closest, for transportation to the Medical Center in Old Forge. Michael hadn't realized that he too had been shot and made no report of it to the Troopers or medical personnel. For several weeks after the incident, his mother would remove shotgun pellets from his back.

Sergeant Wayne Martin, the acting Zone Commander, was doing field inspections when he received a radio message to call the New Hartford station via phone forthwith. It was approximately 6:30 p.m. at that time. Trooper Schreck, assigned to desk duty on this evening, did not want to inform Martin by radio of the shooting. He knew the press would be listening and would descend on the area prematurely and deluge the station with unnecessary phone calls at a time when all the lines should be kept open. Martin instructed Schreck to advise Sr./Inv. Gildersleeve of the State Police Bureau of Criminal Investigation (BCI), Zone Commander Lieutenant Mike Mullins and (acting Troop

Commander), Captain George Loomis. Schreck also called Chief of Police Bob Crofoot of the Town of Webb to assist.

Officer Martin activated his red lights and siren and headed into the Adirondack Park at breakneck speed. He had an hour of travel to reach the Big Moose Road and would have to go a bit out of his way to stop at the Health Center in Old Forge. His first thought was how to block the northern approach to Moss Lake. To do that, he would have to risk an officer's life by having him drive past the Indian bunkers in order to position himself north of the Mohawks' encampment. There had been no subsequent shootings, but he still had to approach this matter carefully before making a snap decision. It sounded like this might be an all out confrontation with the Indians, which had been predicted by many. The State Police helicopter was not an option as it was prohibited from flying during the hours of darkness. Officer Sehring was stopping traffic from traveling north on the Big Moose Road, but there would be many cars north of the Indians that would be returning from Big Moose, which would head south through the Mohawks encampment to reach Eagle Bay.

Martin advised the deskman at New Hartford to have the State Police Lowville car head towards Moss Lake from Stillwater over the nearly impassable wagon trail of a roadway to affect a roadblock at the northern end of the Big Moose Road. The Lowville Troopers were over an hour away and who knew that wagon trail of a road could be blocked by a tree or some other unknown object. He also thought to ask for help from civilians that resided north of Ganienkeh. But, he quickly discounted that as an option.

He had not received any orders from superiors, which meant that this one was his to make or break. This seemed to be the rule in the State Police, the ranking member at the scene made the calls. For just a moment Martin's mind took him back to the 1800's when the pioneers heading west would "circle their wagons" when an Indian attack was imminent. He quickly returned to reality and thought to himself, "I wonder if maybe we ought to start circling our wagons."

In order to verify the complaint, Martin briefly stopped at the Old Forge Medical Center where he was met by Trooper Al Smith and Chief Crofoot. It was about 7:45 p.m. when he arrived. The victim, who was in serious condition, had been treated and was being prepared for transfer to the Saint Lukes Trauma Center in Utica, New York. Martin very briefly interviewed the Drakes. The bullet had penetrated Stephen's left shoulder and chest cavity. I.V's were administered to Drake while en route to the hospital and he was accompanied by Dr. Phil Eathoff, who administered techniques to slow the loss of blood. That fact turned out to be, perhaps, the life saving decision made by medical personnel at the Medical Center in Old Forge. When approximately fifteen miles south of Old Forge, the passengers in the ambulance began to notice a rumbling noise and the vehicle began vibrating. The operator pulled to the side of the road and as he expected, the rear tire on the vehicle was flat. Now, in addition to the physical trauma Stephen was feeling, as his wounds continued to bleed, he wondered if he might bleed to death before they reached the St. Luke's trauma center. This was the most frightening moment for him since the shooting. After an additional fifteen minutes, to the relief of everyone on board, the tire was replaced and the ambulance was able to continue its journey to Utica. Upon his arrival at the hospital, Drake was given seven units of blood to stabilize his condition.

Trooper Smith and Chief Crofoot had also interviewed the Drakes prior to Martin's arrival. The brothers both adamantly denied firing at the Indians first. The Troopers made a cursory search of the car knowing that they were badly needed on the Big Moose Road. There was no sign of empty cartridge casings or weapons in the vehicle. At this point, the officers were convinced that they were investigating the attempted murder of the Drakes. There was no time to conduct a thorough search of the auto and it didn't seem prudent to impound a victim's car, at least not at this point. That would just have to wait until things settled down and more officers were brought into the area.

The trio of officers quickly traveled to the Sehring residence on the Big Moose Road, making it their temporary command post. Trooper Smith relieved Sehring on the roadway, rerouting traffic back towards Eagle Bay.

Lt. Mike Mullins had just arrived and entered the command post when gunfire erupted outside the trailer. Zone Sergeant Martin who was in position, drew his .357 magnum from its holster and cautiously exited the trailer to ascertain if the Indians had attacked. He wondered why it seemed unusually dark outside the trailer. He returned shortly with the hint of a smile on his face. He stated, "Not to worry it was only Smitty (Trooper Smith) shooting out street lights. Didn't want to be an easy target for the Indians." Smith was a huge target with or without street lights. He was six foot five and a rugged two hundred fifty pounds of north woods muscle. He was nicknamed "Big Foot" by the Police Officers of the area.

The officers realized that Barny Barnum, the caretaker of Camp Gorham, (a YMCA boy's camp) would be in position to stop the cars from driving past the Indian stronghold. Barny was also a part time Conservation Officer during the Big Game hunting season and because of this would not be considered a civilian. After a short period of time, Barnum was contacted via phone. He agreed to help until the arrival of the Lowville Troopers and proceeded to stop the traffic from going south. What the trio of officers didn't realize was that they were already too late. It was 8:30 p.m., and while they attempted to close the road, another car drove into the teeth of the runnin' gears of hell. It was the Madigans from Geneva, New York.

The Madigans were vacationing in the area and had visited the Glenmore Hotel in Big Moose for dinner. They had already been spooked by tails of murder on Big Moose Lake and were anxious to get out of the area. They had not heard of the Indian takeover of the Moss Lake Girls' Camp and had no notion of the danger that lurked, as they drove past the encampment. When they reached the area of the two bunkers on the west side of the roadway, they found themselves in the middle of a military type barrage of gunfire. Luckily, the car was not disabled and they sped from the scene towards Eagle Bay. Roger Madigan did not know what was happening, but he knew he had to get away from the chaos, fearing that the aggressors would be chasing them with their cars. This car too, had been riddled with bullets from fully automatic weapons, rifles, and shotguns. Even though it was hard to shoot in darkness, the Indians were quite accurate, striking the car a minimum of six times. Little Aprile Madigan, age nine, lay on the back seat, blood running down her back onto the cushions of the car. She called to her dad, "Daddy I think I'm going to die."

Driving as fast as he could to get away, Madigan reached the roadblock at the edge of Eagle Bay, stopping for help from the officers there. Aprile was put in a State Police Cruiser with three officers. Her mom, Jean, sat on an officer's lap in the back seat. Steven, Aprile's older brother, rode in the front, sitting on a Town of Webb officers lap. Roger Madigan remained behind to give his accounting of the tragedy. Trying hard to hold back her tears, Jean attempted to comfort her daughter and assure her that she would live and that she was not seriously injured. There was no time to waste. Aprile's life was in jeopardy and everyone knew it.

At the Old Forge Medical Center, the little girl was treated by the physician on call and promptly put into an ambulance with medical personnel and headed for the Saint Luke's Trauma Center, in Utica, New York. I.V's were administered while en route. Another act of attempted murder had occurred, this time against the Madigans.

Denny McCalister, a resident of Big Moose, was following the developments very closely as they unfolded, when he learned that a Watertown, New York T.V. station was broadcasting that a nine year old Indian girl had been shot at Ganienkeh. The time was shortly after nine o'clock and it appeared that the reporter had jumped the gun, no doubt picking up pieces of information while monitoring the State Police radio system. McCalister called the reporter via phone and chastised him for reporting the incorrect information, demanding a retraction. The reporter immediately broadcast a correction of his story along with an apology to his viewing audience. From that point on, he worked very closely with the residents of Big Moose and developed an excellent rapport and relationship with them.

Aprile had received two bullet wounds to her back and was listed in critical condition. One piece of the bullet was lodged near her heart and was so close that its removal would surely result in her death. It appeared that the armor piercing round had penetrated the trunk, hitting the rim on the spare tire, where it had split in two; each piece had entered Aprile's body on either side of her spine. Emergency surgery involved an exploratory of her abdomen which revealed the damage the projectile had done. Removal of a large part of her intestines was necessary and doctors feared that she could suffer possible kidney and liver damage. Dr. Lester Eidlehock was her attending physician and surgeon.

The child lingered near death in the hospital for days, and after learning that the Indians had shot her, she developed nightmares, waking up in the middle of the night screaming that the Indians were after her. They were at the windows and in the hall; they were everywhere. Shades and curtains in her room had to be kept drawn at all times and even the sound of people walking in the hallway spooked her.

After approximately a month, she was allowed home for Thanksgiving. After three additional months of recovery time to gain strength, she returned to St. Lukes for the removal of the bullet lodged by her heart. The surgery was successful and Dr. Lester Eidlehock was the surgeon and attending physician once again.

A puzzling aspect of the Madigan shooting was this: Why did the young braves single out the Madigan car if the Madigans did not harass them first? After all, between the times the Drakes had been shot and the Madigan car approached Ganienkeh, probably no less than twenty five other cars had passed without incident. One theory is that Doug Bennett, the future President of COPCA (Concerned Persons of the Central Adirondacks), had been somewhat of a thorn in the side of the Mohawks and was very outspoken concerning their occupation of Moss Lake. Unfortunately for the Madigans, the Bennett's drove a similar Chevrolet Caprice. Very possibly in the darkness, the Indians had mistaken the two cars. Their target may really have been Doug and Bonnie Bennett. A second theory emerged that the Madigan car was mistaken for another vigilante's car. This was very possible as the roadway was dark in the area of the shooting and other vigilantes were operating in the area beside the Drakes.

It was now 10:00 p.m. and the firehouse in Eagle Bay was full of Troopers and Town of Webb Policemen. Off duty Troopers, even some who were on vacation, who lived within a couple of hours of Eagle Bay responded to assist the on-duty members, bringing their personal firearms with them. The acting Troop Commander, Captain George Loomis was present at the new command post. The Captain, Lieutenant Mullins, and Zone Sergeant Martin, let it be known that they were headed to the Indian encampment in an effort to stop the needless shooting. They called the Indians by phone and advised them that Troopers were coming to the gate. Trooper Smith asked if he could accompany the trio. The captain replied, "You fool you're retiring in a few days. Why now?" Smith jumped into the back seat of the Captain's car, disregarding the advice he had just received.

While en route up the Big Moose Road towards Moss Lake, Martin couldn't help but notice that the Captain, George Loomis, looked an awful lot like the pictures he had seen of General George Custer of the infamous "Little Big Horn Massacre." They were quite handsome, with curly blonde hair. Silently Martin hoped that history was not about to repeat itself. As they neared the Ganienkeh gate, Martin made note of the moon shining onto the shards of glass on the roadway. A reminder of what had happened there to the victims a short time before. It gave him chills and made him wonder of what might lay ahead for the officers and the local residents.

As they exited the State Police Cruiser, they were immediately encircled by eight or nine young warriors carrying deer rifles. In the absence of Arthur Montour (Kakwirakeron), the Mohawk's spokesperson, and any of the Chiefs, they were met by a middle age Indian Male who identified himself as "Sawantis." Captain Loomis, in a very forceful way, quickly got to the point, stating, "Cut this shit out. Did you know that you just shot a nine year old girl?" No visible reaction could be ascertained on the faces of the young braves, as the area was very dark. The officers tried to get as close to the Indians as possible to smell their breath, but they could not detect any alcohol and none of the Warriors appeared intoxicated. The Indians agreed to a temporary cease fire for the night but were adamant that State Police would not be allowed to investigate on the sovereign land of Ganienkeh.

As they drove back towards Eagle Bay, Martin had time to check the moon, which he would have bet was full, but it wasn't. There would be three more days before that would occur. In that era, officers believed that on nights of the full moon people did strange things and very unusual happenings such as flying saucers were observed. The Indians and the vigilante's didn't need a full moon.

Senior Investigator Dick Gildersleeve and several other Troopers met the victims at Saint Lukes Hospital, taking verbal statements from them there. He then saw to it that both vehicles were thoroughly searched for any indication that firearms had been discharged within. The search was negative in both vehicles, and there was no evidence of the Drakes giving any false information. At a later date, both Drakes were given a polygraph test, which both passed. Gildersleeve was assigned as the lead investigator on the case by Major Robert Charland.

While inspecting the victim's cars over and over again, the Troopers observed a very interesting bullet hole pattern. For the most part the bullets had entered from the rear, except for the one that struck Drake, which was fired from in front and above the car. The trajectory of the bullet that struck Drake entered through the left side of the windshield and headed downward into his shoulder, making that fact perfectly clear. Aprile Madigan, who was seated in the back of the car, was struck from behind. There was an Indian firing at the Madigan car from the front as well. One projectile was found lodged in the firewall in back of the motor which had entered from the front of the car. Had it not stopped it would have struck Jean Madigan in her mid section. It would seem that common sense might dictate that the Indians opened fire only after the vehicles had gotten past their position, except, of course, the brave that shot Drake from the front and the one bullet that penetrated the Madigan car from the front and lodged in the firewall. What did this mean? 1. That the Indians who allege they were previously harassed that evening were slow to recognize the Drake car returning from Big Moose, and commenced shooting only after the vehicle had passed, making sure that it was indeed the Drakes. 2. That most of the young Indians did not mean to cause injury but only to return the harassment with force. 3. That there was harassment and/or possible gun fire from the autos and that the braves would have had less than five seconds to return fire at the side and rear of the cars as they passed, then continuing to fire at the rear of the escaping autos once they had gotten by the Warrior gauntlet. The intent of the Indians and the motivation for each shooting is probably different. Without a proper on scene investigation, including interviews of the braves that were there, the exact truth may never be known. But there was at least one brave firing a thirty five millimeter weapon whose intent was to kill, and this should be considered attempted murder of six people.

The following day was one of apprehension; the Troopers did not know what the Mohawks would do next. Truly a day to circle the wagons in case of further attacks, which the locals were afraid would occur. Most people in the area who learned of the shooting brought out and loaded their firearms for quick access, and they made sure their doors and windows were locked. They were transported back in time to the 1800's by what was happening around them. They could feel the same type of fear that the pioneers had endured when in Indian country. Those who had children that traveled to school by bus and ride past the Indians initially kept their children home until State Troopers commenced escorting the buses that traveled past the Mohawk encampment. Fear had spread throughout the White and Indian communities like "pollen in the wind," and where ever it would land it would take root and grow.

New arrivals in the Town of Webb were Troop Commander, Robert Charland of the New York State Police, First Sergeant Fred Fessenger, and the radical civil rights Attorney William Kunstler, who had represented the Indians of the Wounded Knee Occupation only months earlier. The Mohawks of Ganienkeh had called him to represent them regarding the two shootings. Then, of course, the press arrived in droves from all over the State. Members of the media that found it too far to travel clogged the phone lines into State Police New Hartford and State Police Oneida (Troop Headquarters). Demands and negotiations had begun.

The meeting place for the representatives was the gate house at the front of the Ganienkeh encampment. It was located just a stone's throw from the Big Moose Road and was the first building on the right side of the driveway. The shack was a small wooden structure with three windows and one door in the front. A small wood burning stove stood in the center of the room, and a series of blankets crudely draped across a clothesline separated the back from the front. Cloth and towels covered the windows, and the room was lit by two kerosene lanterns projecting rays of flickering light on the wooden board walls. It didn't matter what the time of day; it was always night time in the meeting house. After entering from the outside sunlight, it took a few minutes for one's eyes to adjust to the new environment, and then a truly eerie feeling would be experienced when the details of the interior became known.

Oren Lyons, Chief of the Onondagas, was brought in to represent the Mohawks at this first session of negotiations with the State Police. The Onondaga Indians cared for the Great Council Fire for the six nation confederacy. The council fire is a symbol used by the Indians to indicate it was the meeting place for the heads of their government. Ironically, the Mohawk Chiefs had sanctioned the Ganienkeh movement on October 26, 1974, just two days before the outbreak of violence. Lyon's advised all parties that the Indians would pattern their talks on the Canandaigua Treaty of 1794 between the U.S. and the six nations of the Iroquois. That treaty, according to Lyons, spelled out how the Whites and the Indians would settle disputes between two sovereign nations. According to the treaty, the Chief's of the six nations and U.S. President were the only ones authorized to do so. The Chief presented the Mohawk's position to the State Police to add muscle to and to drive home their previous claims of being sovereign. Further, this was an opportunity to enlighten the press regarding all of their past complaints of harassment by the vigilantes of the area.

Article 7 of the Canandaigua Treaty of 1794 reads as follows: "Lest the firm peace and friendship now established should be interrupted by the misconduct of individuals, the United States and the Six Nations agree, that for injuries done by individuals on either side, no private revenge shall take place; but, instead thereof, complaint shall be made by the party injured, to the other: By the Six Nations or any of them, to the President of the United States, or the Superintendent by him appointed: and by the Superintendent, or other person appointed by the President, to the principal Chiefs of the Six Nations, or of the Nation to which the offender belongs; and such prudent measures shall then be pursued as shall be necessary to preserve our peace and friendship unbroken; until the Legislature (or Great Council) of the United States shall make other equitable provisions for the purpose." To the Troopers this was ridiculous. This land belonged to the State and was not an Indian Reservation. A crime had been committed and the State Police were sworn to uphold all laws of New York State.

Major Charland demanded that the Warriors responsible for the shooting be turned over to the State police for questioning. The Indians steadfastly refused this request, pointing out that the State Police did not have the authority to investigate while continuing to maintain that the Whites had fired on the Indians first. They did not, however, deny that they had caused the injuries. The Indian's attorney, William Kunstler, cautioned the State not to reject the Indians' policy. "I have a strong feeling that the Indians would put up resistance and that would be a terrible mistake," he said. "Waiting was the best position at Wounded Knee and it would be here." (Associated Press 10/31/74).

The Warrior Society was given an ultimatum to comply with the investigation. If not, in two hours the police would return and use force. No Indians left the encampment. One woman stated: " There are worse ways for our children to die than from State Police Bullets," referring to drug use and alcoholism on the Indian reservations.

The threat was made in an effort to intimidate the Mohawks into allowing an investigation into the unnecessary shootings. The Troopers did not enter the camp as they had threatened. Charland later stated, "We will not kill women and children just to prove that might makes right." But the fact that the Troopers did not enter the camp gave muscle to the Warriors claim of sovereignty.

The Mohawks now feared that an attack was imminent by the Troopers and they had to prepare as quickly as possible for the assault they believed was coming. The news of the shooting event quickly spread throughout the Indian Nations of the United States and Canada. Many thought that this was "Wounded Knee" all over again.

In an effort to appease the State and the local residents, and no doubt out of fear, the Chief's of the Iroquois quickly announced that they would conduct their own investigation into the shootings, including all of the previous acts of harassment towards the Indians at Ganienkeh. They would make public their findings around Christmas of 1974 and turn them over to the President of the United States. Initially, they even agreed to include the State Troopers in a partial role in the so called investigations, although this never materialized. In the mean time, the Indians prepared, forthwith, to further fortify their mountain stronghold.

Charland ordered two roadblocks on Route 28, the only artery going through the mountainous region. Roadblock one was at Route 28 and the Moose River Road in the hamlet of McKeever. Roadblock two was on Route 28 just to the northeast of Eagle Bay. Those that wanted to get in or out of the area in between the roadblocks were searched and identified. This continued for ten days and no doubt kept many subjects out that wanted in, and many in that wanted out.

Shortly after the roadblocks were set up, a group of students from Cornell University, Ithaca, New York, made arrangements with the Mohawks at Ganienkeh, to bring in a truck load of supplies for the mounting Indian problems. Cornell had a study program of Native American Culture, and when they learned of the happenings at the Moss Lake Mountain Stronghold and heard that many more Indians would be arriving to assist their brothers, they wished to become involved, as they were deeply sympathetic to the Indians' cause.

On the date of the supply delivery, after learning that the students were coming, Captain George Chromey and Zone Sergeant Wayne Martin were at the road block to observe and supervise. The meeting time was set for 8:00 p.m., which was well-observed by the Indians, but the students were forty five minutes late. The braves showed signs of aggravation and were about to leave when a big yellow truck arrived followed by six Volkswagen Bugs loaded with students. They exited (crawled out) the vehicles and went up to the Mohawks, who would not acknowledge them at first, but ignored their presence, no doubt because they were late and had made the Indians wait. Finally, the Mohawks asked who was in charge. The driver of the truck stepped forward and gave the Indian the Peace sign, (a V with two fingers extended upward). One of the Mohawks stated, "I don't have time for that shit. Give me the keys to the truck." The Trooper detail took the keys from the student and inspected the contents of the truck for contraband and/or stowaways. Finding everything in order, the keys were turned over to the braves. The Indians told the students that they could pick up their truck in two days at the same time and warned them not to be late. It seemed the students were beginning to realize that they would not get into Ganienkeh with the supplies as they had been promised. They believed that their arrangement with the Mohawks was to accompany the supplies and help to set up the camp so they could get extra credit for their efforts. Even if the Mohawks would have allowed this, the State Police would have put a stop to it because of the dangers involved (taking hostages etc.) The head Indian, in a very curt manner, stated, "There is no way you are getting into Ganienkeh." By then the students understood that they would not only lose their rented truck, but the deal they had struck with Ganienkeh was not going to materialize. Panic set in and the students asked the Troopers to get the truck back for them and nix the whole deal. At this point, the Indians had already left with the truck and supplies. One of the Troopers stated, "You gave it to them willingly and there's not much we can do now." The students all stuffed into the V.W. Bugs, cramming the extra three that rode in the truck somewhere in the cars and headed over the hill to Cornell University, some one hundred miles to the south. They were no doubt very scared and disappointed because they were responsible for the rented truck.

As promised, two nights later the Mohawks arrived at the road block at 8:00 p.m. with the empty truck. The braves complained to the troopers that the supplies in the truck were "just junk" and mostly useless. Shortly thereafter, one V.W. Bug drove up from the south with two occupants. The students received the keys to the truck from the Indians. The Warriors said "thanks" again in a curt way and headed back towards Ganienkeh. Sergeant Martin asked the driver of the yellow truck when the next shipment would be coming? With a disgusted look on his face, he replied, "that's it man" and drove off towards Cornell University.

Drawing of flag of Ganienkeh by Karoniaktajeh (Louis Hall)

State Police and town of Webb Roadblock

Photograph of Major Robert Charland of NYSP and Indian Mike Mier at beginning of negotiations.

Pictured: Chief Robert (Bob) Crofoot of the Town of Webb PD.

INDIANS POW WOW — Mike Mier, left, and Kakwirakeron, two of the Moss Lake Indians as they discussed their problems yesterday after the shooting of two people on Monday caused State Police to seal off the area.

Chapter 9

Camp Defiance And The Plastic Palace

Immediately after the shooting of Aprile Madigan and Stephen Drake, a plan was drawn up by the State Troopers with input from Chief Bob Crofoot of the Town of Webb Police Department to insure that a recurrence of this nature would never again happen. It was decided by the planners, that there had to be two outposts, one north and one south of Moss Lake, manned by Troopers twenty four hours a day.

Outpost one was located on Big Moose Road in the Hamlet of Eagle Bay approximately two miles south of the Moss Lake Encampment. It was called "Camp Defiance" by the Troopers. Outpost two was located approximately two miles north of the encampment on Big Moose Road at intersection with Higby Road. It was lovingly named the "Plastic Palace" by the Troopers stationed there. There were no other roads in between and any car traveling the Big Moose Road would be under observation of the State Police or Town of Webb Police Department.

This would require the assignment of eight troopers for a twenty four hour period. On the A line (11PM till 7AM), two troopers on each post. During the B line (7AM till 3PM), one trooper on each post. During the C line (3PM till 11PM), one trooper on each post for a total of eight troopers each day. With that number taken from within zone one each day, the coverage to the general public would be severely compromised within the three county area. It was decided that the eight Troopers a day would be taken from each of the three zones of Troop "D". When off duty, the troopers were housed at the Sunset and 19th Green Motels in Old Forge.

After nearly three years of the Indian occupation of Moss Lake, the cost to New York State in trooper salaries, per diem, motel charges and transportation was over one million dollars. But when the media would inquire as to the cost to State taxpayers, the financial section of the State Police in Albany quoted unrealistic figures, leaving out the total cost of salaries (benefits), lodging, transportation, supervision and per diem for the Troopers.

At first, the Troopers at these posts were confined to the troop cars, close to their radios. However, the Troopers and supervisors realized that sitting in police vehicles made them very vulnerable to any aggressive action, particularly during the hours of darkness. Further, with winter approaching, it was a bad idea to sit in the cars for eight hours with the engines idling. Carbon monoxide poisoning was always a threat and had already been experienced in the zone. One trooper died and another was seriously debilitated sitting and watching traffic in Herkimer, New York. The State Police did not want another incident of this nature. The posts were equipped with a Department of Conservation (DEC) radio (SP 7) and a similar radio at State Police New Hartford. This new move provided a backup radio system and immediate contact with Conservation personnel should the need arise. At a later time, phone service was installed so that the Troopers could talk directly with the Indians.

The Zone Lieutenant and Zone Sergeants wrote specific orders for the Moss Lake personnel, outlining what was expected of their men. The officers quickly learned that they were to ignore violations of law on or near Ganienkeh committed by the Indians, and to tolerate violations committed by the local people anywhere in the nearby hamlets. This word of mouth policy just seemed to evolve and no questions were asked by the Troopers. Nowhere in those written orders were the men told not to enforce the law with regard to the Indians. It was just known by all and accepted that no arrests of Mohawks would be made on or near Ganienkeh territory. Outside of Ganienkeh, arrests would be discretionary, and normal good judgment should be used. If doubt was created by some extenuating factor, personnel were to call Zone or Troop Headquarters for orders. These directions were known as "silent orders." Next on the list of things to do was how to house the Troopers on Post?

The Department of Environmental Conservation donated a small six by eight wooden shack of the type used at deer checkpoints during the hunting season. It was installed at outpost one, "Camp Defiance." No toilet could be installed as there was no septic tank. It was equipped with phone service and electricity.

A new innovative, waterless, space-age toilet was being advertised on the market. The State sprung for the purchase of this portable propane gas commode. After its use the patron would have to follow a complicated procedure to burn the matter within. This process was so involved that Gallo wrote a two page memorandum on its use, so that the hairy legged men (no women in those days) would not get anything singed and/or burned. This was reported to have already happened to someone, although no one ever came forward. That phantom report was the reason Gallo wrote the memorandum. Even an explosion was a possibility. It did though, have an upside: When its exhaust spewed like an old coal fired locomotive, the smoke helped to curtail the mosquito problem around the post. The wooded area adjacent to the trailer was not exactly private, as it was just outside the residential area of Eagle Bay and many homes were close by. Members assigned to this post got their bladders stretched as only the bravest used this modern day John. The Troopers quickly named the apparatus the "Jet Shitter." Because it was not used for Natures call, some of the men contemplated using it to boil potato's and/or warm their food, but thought better of the idea after coming to their senses. To this day, no one in Troop "D" will admit to purchasing this unit and no one knows its whereabouts. The memorandum requesting its purchase has disappeared.

Post #2, the Plastic Palace, was another matter. There was no electricity or phone service to be had, but it was very private. It was setup at the intersection of Big Moose Road and Higby Road. Communications between posts was accomplished via car radio. Barny Barnum again came to the aid of the State Police, along with some of the local people of COPCA, manufacturing a really ugly structure made of 2x4 wood framing and plastic wrap insulation material, hence the name "Plastic Palace." Inside was a pot belly wood stove, a gas refrigerator and two old chairs. The floor was mother earth, so it was okay to spill coffee or other liquids on it. It served its purpose and became a meeting place for locals who would bring the troopers coffee and wood for the stove. There they would hash over the latest gossip. Visiting supervisors refrained from looking into the refrigerator for obvious reasons. Supervisors at various times, particularly holidays, would visit the posts with a few large t-bones and all the trimmings. The beef would be charcoal grilled and served with salt potatoes. Perhaps a touch of libation in the form of wine would also be included.

After the first winter, firewood did not come into the plastic palace as fast from the locals. The Big Moose people were obviously getting tired of doing things that were directly the result of the Indian incursion. Nights were getting down to twenty five and thirty below zero for weeks on end. One winter day, Zone Sergeant Gallo picked up Chief Crofoot to discuss recent developments and to check the outposts. The northern post was all but out of firewood for their pot belly stove. The Chief thought that he could locate some wood if there was someone to cut and transport it. The following day, while on pass, Gallo teamed up with Crofoot, and with two chain saws and two pickup trucks, the two officers proceeded to Payne's Saw Mill. The owner, Sid Payne, had given them a pile of slab wood that could be cut up for firewood. It was hardwood and would be long burning. The two officers spent the day cutting the firewood, loading it onto their trucks, and transporting it to the northern outpost, unloading and piling it there. The energy crisis was over for the remainder of that winter.

It was this sort of cooperation between agencies that made the assignment a genuine happy experience for the Troopers and the members of the Town of Webb P.D... This sort of police togetherness kept morale high at all times, although some of the press attempted to portray a different picture to serve their own agenda. This example of cooperation was a stellar display of how two agencies with the same goals could function, and it displayed what most communities could only hope for today.

The Old Forge Station only had two troopers assigned there, but were given the orders to patrol between the two outposts as much as possible and to accompany the school buses that daily traveled the Big Moose road. On the days when there were not enough troopers to follow the buses, the Town of Webb Police Department would once again augment the trooper patrols. Additionally the Troopers agreed to escort essential vehicles through the area to supply the local hotels and businesses.

Indian Givers

A photograph appeared in a local paper and captioned "Troopers Escort Essential Vehicles by Ganienkeh." It was a Utica Club beer truck with two Troopers riding shotgun in a State Police car. We have to wonder if that truck also stopped at the outposts for a moment while en route to Big Moose. The local people most certainly received a chuckle over the picture. No one at the Zone office remembered sanctioning this sort of delivery, but, in retrospect the beer was essential for the operation of the Inns and hotels in the Big Moose area.

The members assigned to the outposts, as well as the local patrols, were required to keep comprehensive records of the day's activity. Trooper Bill Chesebro was noted for keeping outstanding notes. He set the example for the other Troopers assigned at the outposts and would periodically check the records for completeness. If one wanted to know who the strangers were that visited Old Forge, Eagle Bay or Inlet, during any preceding day or night, Bill's notes probably would provide the answer. These records kept by the troopers proved to be invaluable. Any strange vehicle on the Big Moose Road was logged in and a data (owner, residence and any wants) was obtained. Wants didn't necessarily mean that a warrant was issued. It could mean that the person was wanted and a warrant would be issued at a later time. In this manner, (the Post records) revealed who and how many Mohawks were within the Moss Lake encampment and who was a wanted subject. If anyone committed a crime on Big Moose Road, the records were almost as good as a video camera. Daily, Investigator Gildersleeve would check the log books for information. The Troopers stationed at Old Forge delivered the completed forms to State Police New Hartford Zone office, where they were reviewed and filed.

These outposts and their grey clad occupants with purple ties, remained for nearly three full years. Their placement there, gave COPCA some security and no doubt relieved some of the anxiety of the area. Additionally, many of the Troopers while off duty and on, made good friends with the people of Big Moose. It must be noted that the outposts' presence and the occupants, no doubt prevented many additional crimes that would have occurred, keeping the Indians and Whites apart. Also, these posts and the presence of the State Police in a neutral posture may have kept another Wounded Knee from erupting.

Nine year old Aprile Madigan in wheel chair is visited in the hospital by children Of Big Moose.

Chapter 10

The Interlopers

The Warrior Society had to believe that by shooting the two youths that they had just poked a stick at a sleeping bear (the State of New York). There is safety in numbers and the Warrior Society was pleased and relieved with the response that came from Indians throughout Canada and the United States when these supporters learned of the Mohawks' problem. Many choose to travel to Moss Lake, believing there would be a government response to the shooting of the two Whites. They arrived in the area with their weapons, expecting a fight. Some who were considered interlopers (un-welcomed guests) because of their baggage (records and outstanding warrants) were not well received at Ganienkeh, but no Indians, traditional or nontraditional, at this time of crisis were refused entry into the encampment. The new comers numbered close to one hundred fifty, all of them armed and ready to fight to defend the Mohawks sovereignty. As they drifted in, the Troopers obtained information from all over the United States and Canada as to who they were and what weapons they were carrying. At one point U.S. Customs advised the State Police that eighteen Indian youths, in one group, had crossed the border into the United States at the Thousand Island bridge.

A.I.M (The American Indian Movement) was well represented by the new arrivals at the encampment. This organization was very militant and radical, best known for their recent involvement in the Wounded Knee confrontation. The most infamous of the Indians reported as arriving at Ganienkeh were:

Dennis Banks, a co-founder of AIM
Clyde Bellecourt, another National leader of AIM
Vernon Bellecourt, another National leader of AIM
Mike Mier, Canadian National Chairman of AIM
(COPCA newsletter of 12/2/74)

Each of these men had militant records of varying degrees, and the question of whether or not they were welcome at Ganienkeh by the Mohawks is one left unanswered. It is believed that at this time the Warriors were trying to distance themselves from the AIM organization and the militant title it carried, but for the moment, they needed their support. At a later date other issues would surface that would answer this question. A wider brush stroke (more investigation) was needed to bring forth other indications of AIM involvement.

The Troopers received numerous reports of militants headed for Moss Lake. One such report told of a militant Mohawk, and another twenty year old Indian male heading for Moss Lake in a red pickup truck full of hand grenades and ammo. Zone Sergeant Gallo, who now spent much of his supervisory time in the Moss Lake area putting out fires, and Barny Barnum of DEC intercepted the truck and searched its contents. Barnum stood guard with his eye on the Indians while Gallo went through the vehicle with a fine tooth comb. They found no weapons amongst the bushels of tomatoes that were dug through by the officer. Unfortunately, many tomatoes were damaged during the search, and much juice found its way to the floor of the pickup. Neither of the Indians turned out to be the indians expected, and the truck was not registered in the expected name. A check of the outposts revealed that the truck had arrived at Ganienkeh before the information was received and the Troopers were a day late. No doubt the hand grenades were already at the mountain stronghold.

Overall, the Troopers did not try to stop the ingress of Warriors into Moss Lake, nor did they attempt to take their weapons, a clear indication that there was no plan to evict the Native Americans by force. If a flatbed truck had arrived with a Sherman tank and two howitzers in tow, it is doubtful that the Troopers would have made any attempt to turn the weapons around. It was apparent that in the absence of any orders to the contrary, confrontations and arrests were to be avoided, except when a serious violation was committed such as the possession of hand grenades, and the arrest would occur some distance from the affected area.

It was now time for the Warriors and the interlopers to sharpen their arrows and fill their quivers. The elders were convinced that the assault on the stronghold would soon occur. They dug ditches and foxholes and destroyed bridges allowing access to Moss Lake. Using cases of dynamite that had been previously transported to the encampment, they made booby traps, the extra buried somewhere in the mountain stronghold, which could now be considered a fortress. Extra sentries were posted day and night, sometimes manning their posts with women and children as well as braves. Among the Indians and Whites of the area, anxiety was at a peek. No one doubted the belief that an attack by the Troopers was imminent. The Mohawks had to believe that the Troopers would pick this time to attack while the many wanted Indians were at the encampment.

On one sunny day when the crisis was still at a peak the Mohawks believed that the invasion had begun when they heard the telltale slapping of large helicopter props approaching Moss Lake from the south. Art Montour called the New Hartford State Police Station in an apparent panic. Was this the time of reckoning? The desk man at New Hartford reassured the Indian spokesman that this was not the start of an assault. A quick call to the DEC revealed that indeed it was a fish stocking episode and that they had made an error when including Moss Lake, Bubb Lake, and Sis Lake in their stocking plans. It is the policy of DEC to stock mountain lakes in the fall with fingerling brook trout. The Choppers were loaded with fish and not Troopers; nonetheless, the fish were dropped in the lake. It is unknown if the Indians fired on the Helicopters. In an interview many years later, Paul Deleronde, who was being interviewed by Brad Lockwood of the New York Press, hinted that he had a habit of shooting at helicopters. Deleronde who was a young brave at the time was at Moss Lake. The State Police instructed the DEC to advise them of any future fish stocking in the Adirondacks well in advance of such action.

As time passed, no attack took place, and negotiations seemed to be improving. The anxiety of the area ebbed and things returned to almost normal, and many of the interlopers slowly returned to their homes in North America. However, some remained and became problems to both the Mohawks and the Troopers at a later time. One group was particularly pleased to see them leave. They were the Mohawk Women, who had to cook and clean for the influx of Warriors. Additionally, they were taking the places of braves as sentries when the Warriors were needed elsewhere.

Chapter 11

Mohawk Women And Children

Without consideration as to whether or not the encroachment by the Mohawks Warrior Society (men and women) was right or wrong, their bravery, zeal and perseverance for three years cannot go unnoticed. Their ability to bear the horrible conditions there at Moss Lake while raising their children under the constant threat of attack can be considered nothing less than heroic. The lack of food and warm shelter, the adverse weather that Mother Nature can deal out in these mountains, and the lack of modern conveniences can make a case for an almost historical parallel with the first settlers' problems at Jamestown during the 1600's. The buildings at Moss Lake were not insulated and provided not much more than wind breakers for the Indians.

Very noteworthy is the willingness of the Warrior Society women, in the first place, to allow this overt act and support the men at Moss Lake for three long years of their lives, when they in fact had the power to nix the whole plan if they felt the risk of life was not worth the gains they might expect. They, the whole society, ventured into years of danger and strife with very little knowledge of what lay ahead of them. It must have been a most dramatic period in the lives of both the women and the children. Where and how would they sleep upon their arrival? Would they be met with gunfire? Were the buildings that were there infested with rodents and/or spiders and snakes? How would they keep warm in the days following? What would they do about sickness and death? They also had to worry about schooling the children, childbirth, gardening, hunting and fishing and cooking for large groups of people.

And how would they cope with the most serious predator of the north woods, the black fly that would attack in swarms during the spring, summer and fall and biting repeatedly if proper precautions were not taken: fly dope and face netting. These insects were attracted to the sweat of a human and if one was allergic, it could mean death. Loggers, hunters, campers and hikers were all plagued by this tiny black insect. At times, the animals of the north woods would be driven into the water to escape the black fly's wrath.

The women of the Warrior Society made and/or helped make the most important decisions of the group, which at that time in history was highly unusual in the thinking of White men and White women. In an interview, Louise Leclair, niece of Louis Karoniaktajeh Hall, stated, "My uncle Louis Karoniaktajeh Hall taught me that the Mohawk women hold a very important role. They have a critical decision-making chip in whatever their people do and were years ahead of the Women's Liberation in recognizing the wealth and power of women. Their role though, does not call for them to pick up arms and fight, mainly because they were the vital source for carrying on the Mohawk blood line. Of course, in the 1970's and after, my uncle was proud to see women who were willing to fight alongside of the men if necessary." Louise continued: "It is the women who hold the title to the land and traditionally if a man were to marry a woman from another Mohawk settlement, he would move to the women's territory and move in with her family. My own grandfather was from Akwesasne and moved to Kanawake to my grandmother's territory when they married. It is the women who have the last and final say when men pick up their weapons and risk their lives, because it is the women who bore those men for nine months, went through the birthing pain and brought the boy/man into the world. It is her say as to whether or not what they are defending is worth giving up the life the women gave them."

After the tragic shooting of a nine year old White girl and a young White male by the Indians, the women and children were told by the Troopers that they had two hours to depart the Moss Lake encampment, as the Troopers were poised to enter by force. A women's meeting was held to determine what action should be taken. They decided that no Indian would leave. "There are worse ways to die than by State Police bullets," the women reportedly said. "We won't send our children back to die of alcoholism and drugs on the reservation." (Sovereignty and Symbol, Landsman, page 30).

Along these same lines, another woman of Ganienkeh who wished to remain anonymous stated, "It's for our children that we're really here. To leave... to go back to the reservation... to give up everything we know is right...there is no way we will ever do that..."

Shortly after the women's decision to remain at Ganienkeh in the face of an attack, Major Robert Charland of the State Police stated: "To enter Ganienkeh would have been a bloodbath to end all bloodbaths, and it would have made Attica look like a Sunday School Picnic" (Sovereignty and Symbol, Landsman 1978). To end the Attica State Prison riots, Troopers shot and killed thirty nine inmates that were holding knives to the hostage's throats. One can only imagine the fear the women had when making the decision to stay at Ganienkeh and possibly face the Troopers in battle. The Mohawk women were brave indeed, but that did not help with their efforts at gardening. Their success at raising crops was meager at best and other than wildlife, the Indians were hard pressed to produce enough food for the many Warriors and their families that settled there. These responsibilities fell on the Mohawk women as well as the men, as everything was a cooperative effort.

There were no modern conveniences other than a telephone and the vehicles they arrived with. These bare essentials pointed to a giant step back in time. Although the Mohawk women were able to travel into the Hamlet of Old Forge on occasion to purchase food, initially money was very scarce. Some funds came from church groups in the Utica/Syracuse area and the newly formed Rights for American Indians (RAIN). Slowly money began to trickle in to help the Mohawks.

Some Whites of the area were critical of the Mohawk women because they would travel into Eagle Bay or Old Forge to do their laundry at the local Laundromat. This was not exactly how traditional Indians were to wash their clothing, the White women felt. Perhaps they expected to see the Indian ladies beating their clothing with rocks at the river or lake edge. In the winter, the lake would be frozen over with two feet of ice, which was hardly conducive to washing clothes. To be truly traditional, the Mohawk Women could have chopped a hole in the ice and carried the water to their homes where it could have been heated to do their wash. But it didn't matter; whether winter or summer, the Indian ladies used the Laundromat, slowly returning to the non-traditional way of life.

During the 25th anniversary celebration at Ganienkeh, then relocated to Clinton County, Robin Caudell, staff writer for the Press Republican in Plattsburgh New York, was able to interview many of the women of the Warriors Society who were there at Moss Lake. Verna Montour (Eintion - "meaning a land of my own") and a spokesperson for the Society, was married to Arthur Montour (Kakwirakeron), also a spokesman for the Mohawks. She said, "The hardest thing for me to learn was to cook on the wood stove for 200 people," referring to the fact that they had no electricity or gas at Moss lake. "We really had to work together, we had to. We were young, we were strong, we could do anything, and we had no fear." She and Kakwirakeron had two of their nine children while at Moss Lake. No medical facility, no doctor, no pain killing drugs, just a midwife. Judy Deleronde (Kasinisake - meaning looking for a name) told Ms. Caudell, "If it moved, they ate it, horse, goat, bear and coon." She recalled once serving a Moss Lake delicacy, "skunk and tea." If one could attach a fancy French name (i.e. escargot for snails) it could catch on. "I wish my husband Oserace could be here." He had died in 1991. "He really believed in the project heart and soul and always helped the women with their chores. I think that is why I stayed after he passed away because I supported him one hundred percent. It's a difficult life style but I adapted. People thought I would leave after the first year."

Because the Indians were portrayed as being very poor and in need of almost everything to exist, there was much criticism of one of the Warrior women: Lorraine Montour and her silver grey Porsche that she sported around the area. Lorraine was thirty five and an attractive brunet with long hair and a slender build. She almost always wore tight jeans, was well made up, and neat. She had been married to Arthur Montour's brother Danny, who had fallen to his death from a high rise building he was working on in New York City. Lorraine had received a settlement, worker's compensation, and social security for this tragedy. But her appearance, the car, etc. pinched the noses of the local ladies. She didn't fit the profile of a poor, poverty stricken traditional Mohawk woman. She became well known because of the manner in which she conducted herself and eventually received national attention when she was interviewed by "Playgirl Magazine." That interview focused mostly on the Indian takeover of Moss Lake and the motives behind the incursion and not her playgirl appearance.

The children for the most part loved Moss Lake, but their lifestyle brought up many questions about the different way the Mohawks' were living compared to their White counterparts that had to be answered. Bonnie Thornton Duff, one of the grass-roots supporters of the Indian movement, recalled Chief Karoniaktajeh (Louis Hall) sitting for hours and answering a group of children's questions. "The children said uncle we have some questions." He sat there and talked to them for two hours. "You might think we talked a long time, but we needed to talk until everyone was finished," the Chief said. For the most part the children wondered why their lifestyle was different from their White friends, and why the Moss Lake encampment was so important to the older Indians.

Donna McCumber, the daughter of Judy Deleronde, was one of the children of Moss Lake. She was ten when her father went to the Mountain stronghold. "I remember my father saying, 'I don't know if I'll be back.' He went and a week later he came back and got us. Moss Lake was beautiful for a kid. You were on your own. We had school periodically," McCumber said. "They had shifts for the girls to wash the dishes. We did dishes for 3 hours. There were stacks and stacks. I'm glad I was there." She further stated, "My father was strict. We all worked. They got us up early in the morning, and we worked in the garden. If you weren't there someone would come and get you. We had to entertain ourselves. We didn't have T.V. There wasn't any Nintendo or computers. I wish I could give that to my kids, so they could learn responsibility."

There were very scary times for everyone there, particularly the children, when they were harassed late at night by unknown parties. The Warriors would respond with gunfire to defend their families and to scare away the intruders. The Mohawk's allege that one day when the children were out on the grounds playing, someone began shooting at them. The children hid behind a rock and yelled that they were kids so the shooter or shooters would stop. The gunfire continued for some time before it ceased, leaving the children quite frightened.

During the occupation of Moss Lake nine babies were born. The cold winter nights and the adventure they were experiencing no doubt resulted in romance, which in turn resulted in nine little Indians. Not all of the babies were born in the traditional manner. In one case, because of complications, the delivery was performed by a doctor who came to the encampment from Old Forge, probably one of a very few white people that got beyond the Ganienkeh gate. It was rumored that a pregnant Mohawk walked from the Dakota's to Ganienkeh just to have her baby born there. He was the first born at the encampment and she named the boy "Flint." But many, including some of the Mohawks, doubted that she had really made the trek.

It becomes very obvious that the women and children experienced a difficult and scary three years at Ganienkeh, a time in their lives that none will forget. But that same period of time, because of the Warrior Society incursion of Moss Lake, caused as much or more difficulty and anxiety in the people of Big Moose and surrounding area. Of course, the attempted murder of the Drakes and the Madigans would be the "coup de grace" of suffering for all.

TROOPERS RIDE 'SHOTGUN' FOR TRUCK — Only essential vehicles were allowed into the Eagle Bay area yesterday. As a result this Utica Club beer truck found itself with a State Police escort as it made deliveries to stores and taverns in the area.

Pictured: Barney Barnum and wife Betty who were indispensible to State Police.

Chapter 12

Salsa In Their Blood

Most were hot and some were not! The local people of Old Forge, Eagle Bay, Inlet and Big Moose were fed up with the State's inaction and the recent shooting of Stephen Drake and Aprile Madigan by the Mohawks. In the area, there was a small group of sympathizers reaching out to other parts of the State for aid for the Indians (money, food, medical supplies and legal representation), but for the most part, the White's were becoming very angry and turning against the Indians.

Immediately after the shooting of Drake and Madigan, a newly formed group of local persons banded together and called themselves, Concerned Persons of The Central Adirondacks (COPCA). After a community meeting, the Big Moose Fish and Game club, the Fire Department and the local property owners unanimously agreed that the Indians had to be removed. They were in fear of further Indian attacks and loss of business. They actually talked of forming their own eviction team and "throwing them out." After a little more rational discussion they realized they would in fact become "vigilantes," and what they were proposing was far from rational. They quickly extinguished the idea. But these thoughts indicate the degree of anger they possessed.

The COPCA board was initially made up of eight persons, with Doug Bennett (owner of the Big Moose Inn) as their president. Other members were Bill Judson, Diane Bowes, Denny McCalister, Barny Barnum, Bob Winters, Butch Cole and Howard Martin. The organization decided it was time to turn up the wick on the politicians of the State.

For the most part, COPCA was made up of citizens from Big Moose and Eagle Bay, with a spattering from Old Forge and Inlet. Their blood was boiling as though salsa was flowing through their veins. They had been patient with the Indian occupation of Moss Lake, waiting for New York State politicians to solve the problem. But their patience grew thin. They became concerned, irritated, and more apprehensive, viewing the future in the area with anxiety and alarm. They even asked the State for escorts by the encampment, but were refused. Only the school buses that traveled the route would be accompanied by a Police Officer. The State continued to ignore the situation and the Indians were given free rein with no fear of enforcement by the State Troopers. In fact, the locals felt that the Troopers were there in service of the Indians rather than the State.

In a statement of principles the group cited its basic goals as:
1. "The return of Moss Lake, Bubb Lake and Sis Lake to the jurisdiction of the State of New York, the owner of the properties. This includes the departure of the Indians from these properties at least until such time as their claims have been adjudicated by proper legal process."
2. "The presentation of facts about the Moss Lake Encampment that are unknown to the general public or facts that have been, due to one thing or another, distorted as to mislead the public."

The eight person COPCA committee charged that "The Indian Movement was well planned, intelligently sequenced, cleverly propagandized and had automatic minority appeal." In a later release to the public, COPCA listed the many acts of the Indians (over thirty) that constituted a violation of law, including the shooting of the two Whites. The members of COPCA stated: "At this point, some obvious questions are raised. Have the civil rights of the traveling public been violated. If you broke as many laws as the occupants of Moss Lake, would you not expect to be subject to legal due process. Why does the action of the State punish the innocent and protect those that have violated the law? Are you as a taxpayer, prepared to lose your land in the Adirondack Park?" (COPCA bulletin 1974a). This age old question of protecting the accused over the injured party has been recognized and debated for ages. Many learned people profess that over time these laws to protect the rights of the accused evolved because they were needed, but protecting the accused also made the fatted calf fatter. The lawyers and judges have been accused of exasperating these laws. The laws that provide for the protection of the accused are never ending and of course written by those that benefit the most. There is no question that the scales of justice have been tipped in favor of the accused.

COPCA was anything but complacent with regard to their issues: Letter writing to politicians and the local papers was the norm, as well as appearing on television and radio programs in nose to nose debates with the Mohawks and reaching out to the local populace with periodical newsletters. Their mailing list grew to over four thousand as the people of New York State learned of the Indian take-over. COPCA asked one basic question: "Why has this state of lawlessness been allowed to continue? The members of COPCA feel that law and order has been prohibited by top state officials from pursuing its proper cause." (COPCA news letter 12/2/74).

One lady and member of COPCA who wished to remain anonymous wrote a scathing letter to Governor Hugh Carey:

> Our son... has most certainly been affected to a great degree by the successful, forceful takeover of land by this group of Indians. He has written to you, along with the comment to us, "Maybe if I tell Governor Cary how we don't like to live here and be afraid, then he'll do something to help us." Innocence is beautiful. With the mind of a youth, it has gone right over his head that so many of our efforts have been directed toward you and your staff in an effort to resolve a pitiful mentally and physically sick situation.
>
> Where have all our heroes gone? What shall we tell our little boys and girls today? Can we honestly teach them as we were taught...to look to our leaders and they will uphold our faith in righteousness? Do you not suppose (whomever may be reading this letter) he has seen movies on T.V. news of these "Moss Lake Indians" flaunting our United States Flag upside down? Do you not suppose his little mind wonders why "The Government, presumably condones this action by allowing this forceful, criminal action to lay dormant for over one year?"
>
> I do not wish to exploit our son. You will not see his letter printed in the newspaper; but, from the outside looking in, God help you all, in governmental positions throughout our United

States, to see and uphold the truth. We've all heard too many "Not now, its election time," or I can't, I have political ambitions and don't want to step on any toes." These comments look as if we've been electing a tremendous number of "social climbing politicians. I don't wish to sound cynical; I wish to say, please open your eyes and look all around you.

This letter was taken from a written critique of Mike Blair's work while employed by COPCA, prepared by him for the members of COPCA.)

Both sides to the dispute (COPCA and the Mohawks), not counting the State, were making full use of the media, with the Indians taking the lead with the sympathy factor they received as a minority. Art Montour, the Mohawk Spokesman, was a master at controlling the press and sympathy rolled in from all parts of the State. In an effort to narrow the gap, in the spring of 1975, COPCA hired Michael Blair, who had been the editor of a small newspaper, "The Lowville Republican." Blair was somewhat controversial and had become involved in a political dispute of his own making, allegedly involving the use of campaign funds in an improper manner by a North Country assemblyman, K. Daniel Haley, a democrat who represented St. Lawrence and Franklin Counties in the Legislature.

The ex-editor had prepared a confidential report regarding the Mohawks' takeover of the Moss Lake Girls' Camp for the sum of $1500, being paid by Haley the North Country politician, out of campaign funds. This report was researched and written prior to his employment by COPCA. The report eventually became public and could be purchased for $20.00. The document ended up in the hands of Senator James Donovan who used it to no end to attack his own government's failure to properly handle the Indian problem.

In Blair's report several problems could be quickly identified: The date of his report was shown as January 6, 1974, five months before the Mohawks' repossession of the Girls' Camp on May 13, 1974. While referring to A Mohawk complaint of an early incident where three White Men came to the front gate of Ganienkeh in an intoxicated state harassing the Indians, Blair contended that the Indians were lying about the men firing their weapon at them. He based this on the fact that six empty rounds were found at the scene. The rounds were from a 44 cal. Ruger Rifle. According to Blair, after checking with the Ruger

Company, he learned that the rifle only held five rounds and there would not have been time to reload by the aggressors. What Blair didn't report, or was not told, was that the Ruger 44 cal. revolver, could be a six round weapon, along with other manufacturers of six gun revolvers, and fired the same magnum cartridge as the rifle. The Indians did not describe the weapon as a rifle or a revolver, probably because it was not seen. Therefore, a possibility exists that the weapon used indeed fired six rounds without reloading, and could have been the weapon fired by the Whites. He then refers to an interview of Investigator Ray Polett of the State Police in Lowville for information and opinions of the Investigator regarding the Moss Lake affair. Although Polett was a highly respected Trooper, he was not directly involved in the Ganienkeh investigation and never assigned there. Then, and most disturbing of all, Blair set out a plan to recover the usurped land by the use of force, a commando type raid using helicopters, dislodging the encroachers in the middle of winter and in the late night hours. This was quite arrogant in that he had no experience as a police officer or to our knowledge the military, and yet was trying to orchestrate a police action that would no doubt result in multiple injuries and death, including the death and injury of Indian children. Not a good way to make friends of the Mohawks.

In spite of his dangerous confidential report, Blair was a hard worker for the COPCA organization, becoming their public relations man and spokesperson. His work, through constant public debates with the Indians, and his constant criticism of the State, drew the organization up to an even playing field with Art Montour and the Mohawks, winning some of the debates on T.V., radio, and on campuses in New York State. As an example, he entered into a radio debate with Montour at WBRV in Boonville, New York. At one point he asked Montour if he could provide the names of the nine Iroquois Chiefs. Montour was unable to provide the names, and became quite embarrassed. Blair felt that this just pointed out that the Warriors were just militant Indians and not true Traditionals. His work also weighed heavily on the State of New York to resolve this very dangerous situation in the area. In July of 1975 Blair prepared a publication announcing free land in the Adirondack Park in an effort to further embarrass the State:

FREE LAND
ATTENTION: MILITANT GROUPS, LIBERATION ORGANIZATIONS AND ANACHIST GROUPS OF ALL TYPES

If your group would like to occupy prime New York State Department of Environmental Conservation land, some complete with winterized buildings, private lakes, snowmobile trails and hundreds of acres of prime forest land…It is available for the taking. To qualify you must provide:
   A. Proof of need to promote your cause
   B. A crusading legal staff
   C. Guns (Rifles, shotguns, automatic
      Weapons preferred - please)

If your group qualifies, the following benefits are yours: N.Y. State Law will remain unenforced. High State Officials will refuse to act, Politicians will run for cover. State Police will protect you. O.E.O. will feed and clothe you.

FOR COMPLETE DETAILS ACT TODAY WHILE PRIME LAND IS STILL AVAILABLE. WRITE OR CALL THE OFFICE OF THE GOVERNOR HUGH CAREY OR COMMISSIONE OF ENVIRONMENTAL CONSERVATION OGDEN REID, STATE CAPITAL, ALBANY, N.Y., AND ASK FOR INFORMATION ON THE MOSS LAKE PACKAGE.

At one point, June of 1975, COPCA appealed to the U.S. Immigration and Naturalization Service in Ogdensburg, New York, Blair demanding that the Indians be sent back to Canada because they were Canadian Indians. Elmer Stark, an official of the agency, said "that the Indians are protected from the immigration laws by the Jay Treaty signed by the United States and England in 1794. The treaty allows the North American Indians to cross the U.S. Canadian border freely and live in either country," he said. (Watertown Daily Times 6/25/75)

On May 9, 1976, COPCA organized a protest demonstration against the Mountain Stronghold of Ganienkeh. Leaders of the march were State Senator James Donovan, Assemblyman William Sears, and Assemblyman Peter Dokuchitz. The Senator and assemblymen said "they were in complete sympathy with the protest and would continue to urge Governor Carey to act on the problem." They also said: "We support COPCA in it's efforts to dramatize the appalling lack of action on the Moss Lake occupation by the state." (Syracuse Post Standard 4/30/75). All three had publically spoken out against the Indian takeover of Moss Lake and applied much pressure on the Governor through the legislature and letter writing, to quickly settle the dilemma.

The demonstration commenced at the outskirts of Eagle Bay and marched north past Ganienkeh until it was out of site of the Mohawks encampment. Approximately 170 people were in the procession carrying placards denouncing the Indian takeover of the land and the inaction of New York State. State Police, in preparation for the protest march met with the Indians and COPCA in an effort to keep everything orderly. Ten additional Troopers were brought into the area to ensure all would go well. But, for the most part, except a few, the Troopers were kept out of sight of the participants, the media and the Indians. A trailer was hidden in the area by the Troopers that contained riot gear (teargas, masks and riot clubs) should they be needed. No incidents of harassment or interference took place, except that as the parade of White's passed the Ganienkeh camp a group of Indians sat on a hill by the road and beat drums and tom toms to drown out the chants of the march. The media was there in full force with a local T.V. Station filming the entire event.

After the procession had rounded the bend passed the encampment, Chief Louis Hall stated that various delegates and Indian supporters got together at a nearby horse corral for additional activities. Kakwirakeron introduced the Indian dignitaries. Representatives of various support groups made speeches; this included the Syracuse Ganienkeh Support Group, Rights for American Indians Now (R.A.I.N.), with delegates from chapters in Binghamton, Clinton, Rochester and other places in New York State. The Native American Solidarity Committee was also represented. According to Chief Louis Hall, "Indians everywhere were delighted to no end. Instead of the Native Americans demonstrating it was their tormentors turn. Even the Senate was represented." (A message from Ganienkeh No.#10, May 11, 1976).

The Mohawks charged that the COPCA organization was racist in its actions. During Doctor Landsman's investigation for her book, Sovereignty and Symbol, in the 1980's, she interviewed one of the organizers of COPCA who wished to remain anonymous, but was quoted as follows: "I have people in Old Forge, very good friends, who insisted as seeing us as an anti-Indian group, as being against these Indians. And as many times as you would tell them that it had absolutely nothing to do with the color of their skin or anything else--- it could be a group of WASP Bishops or whatever----but we didn't feel it was fair that they should be treated one way and we should be treated another way. You know when you sort of see your system of justice breaking down around you, it gives you a real cause of concern." (Landsman 119)

During the summer of 1975 COPCA (Mike Blair) took a calculated risk and unveiled a plan to "ease the tension and resolve the crisis" caused by the occupation of Moss Lake by the Warrior Society. He was offering through a massive fund raising effort of COPCA and Indian benefactors, to purchase 1,365 acre plot on Tug Hill for $135,000 for a relocation territory for the Mohawks. The land was conducive to agriculture with a good water supply and timber. Secretly, he felt that there would be no participation and held his breath until he was proven right. Blair challenged the various groups supporting the Indians: "Today we are calling upon all groups supporting the Indians, and opposing them as well, to join with COPCA in obtaining this land for a traditional Native American territory, to live on in any manner they so desire, as long as its peaceful." (Watertown Times 10/30/75) Again this was done to embarrass the State and to show that COPCA was trying to resolve the situation through peaceful means. The Indians refused the generous offer and got Blair and COPCA off the hook. The Mohawks had something larger and better in mind than a remote piece of land on Tug Hill famous for brutal amounts of lake effect snow and the coldest spot in New York State. What they envisioned was near the Canadian border and close to their old home of Kanawake and Akwesasne (St. Regis). We have to wonder why the Indians quickly turned down the land on Tug Hill without hardly any consideration. Could it be that they had been promised, from the onset, the land along the Canadian border and/or something of greater importance?

Chapter 13

Much Much Wampum

To an Indian "Wampum" can mean much more than money. It can mean legal documents (i.e. deeds, trusts, certificates, family lineage and even be Indian Law etc.), and also tell a story. Some dictionaries still say that it is a form of Indian money with no further reference to its many other uses. Wampum was sacred to the Iroquois and was first introduced by Hiawatha when he formed the Iroquois Nation.

In the case of Ganienkeh, the locals believed that the Mohawks were after cold hard cash, which they thought would be a big part of their settlement with the State. But, any gift, land or money would constitute a major problem because the New York State Constitution forbade anything of value to be given to private individuals. This fact severally complicated the negotiations.

Immediately after the shooting of the two Whites, negotiations of sort began between the State Police and the Warrior Society. Major Charland represented the state and Art Montour, Louis Hall and Mike Mier represented the Indians. Mier was the past leader of the Canadian AIM organization. These early negotiations were made up mostly of complaints by the Mohawks of police harassment, which served to dampen down the escalating crisis and a way to handle complaints that came up.

Charland needed eyes and ears in the Moss Lake area, but no supervisors or investigators were stationed or lived close enough for that role. He turned to Trooper Bill Chesebro, who resided in the Old Forge area and was privy to most all gossip and happenings that took place. Bill's reputation was excellent amongst the locals and he had worked with Charland early on in their careers. Therefore, the major was familiar with the excellent work and loyalty that Chesebro exhibited. An additional factor Charland considered was that Bill had established a rapport with the Mohawks and was respected by them as well. The trooper agreed to be contacted both on and off duty and to resolve any issue that came up if at all possible. Charland designated him as "liaison" to the Mohawks and COPCA.

This assignment did not sit well with the supervisors of the zone, due to Chesebro's new role. The "Chain of Command" was being circumvented and all items of an Indian nature were not being funneled through zone headquarters. At one point, the Zone Commander had become upset with Chesebro's actions and forcefully asked him: "Trooper who do you think you are working for)? Chesebro's reply was: "The major sir." This angered the Lieutenant, but he knew major Charland had his finger on the pulse of the Indian problem because of Chesebro. At a time of crisis, this was a necessary move. This position made it very difficult for Chesebro to deal with zone headquarters and his superiors. The situation no doubt influenced his career a great deal and was quite awkward, but he managed well. Bill never aspired to be promoted, and loved the work of running his own little station and providing police protection for his patrol area and the State as needed. When called in to sign his performance ratings at the Zone office, he would never read the report but would just sign it and walk out

At about this time, Scott Buckheit from the American Arbitration Association, became the local representative, and came on board to assist in the immediate area. He worked very closely with Bill Chesebro, and both helped, not only to move the negotiations forward, but also to solve little matters of aggravation between the parties. Zone supervisors didn't need to travel to Moss Lake each time a complaint was made that could be handled nicely by Chesebro. Although Bill worked many overtime hours on the Indian problem, he did not receive any compensation for his overtime and never asked.

The Indians from the beginning espoused that they would not and could not negotiate with the state because they, the Mohawks, were a sovereign nation and being a country, they could only deal directly with the United States. When the Mohawks ask to meet with the state for the first session on January 28, 1975, it was somewhat of a surprise to the negotiations unit, and viewed as a major step forward in the controversy. The question became, why did the Warrior Society suddenly change direction and agree to negotiate with the State? Is it possible that a very secret arrangement was made between the federal government, the State, and the Indians, which would allow the feds to negotiate with the Mohawks through the State Representatives? In other words: Charland, Cuomo and Rowley may have been used as puppets by the U.S. Government, the puppeteers. The State Police were aware that their Commander was constantly in Washington D.C. during the time of the negotiations that he frequently called from there, or had to be called at different capitol area numbers. This scenario would make a great deal of sense because the Federal Government did not want to recognize Ganienkeh as Sovereign, and if they directly negotiated with the Mohawks, it could mean just that.

They would set a dangerous precedent and somewhat validate the Indian claim of nationhood. This scenario would explain why the Mohawks suddenly agreed to work with the State when in the beginning they proclaimed that it was not a State problem, and that they could only negotiate with the President of the United States or the United Nations. They, the Indians became privy to something? It looked very much like Cuomo, Charland, and Rowley were marching to the beat of distant drums, or tom toms, originating somewhere down by the Potomac.

This first meeting was held in Albany with the New York State Assembly subcommittee, Major Charland and Environmental Commissioner Ogden Reid. It was supposed to be held in secret, but COPCA quickly uncovered its existence. It was agreed between the two parties that this meeting would not involve the legal issues of the 1794 treaty (Canandaigua) or the 1797 treaty concerning the Mohawk's claim of nine million acres of upstate New York and all of the State of Vermont. It became a complaint session wherein the Indians could vent their most recent grievances.

It seemed that the most important issue to the Mohawks was the return of a silver gray Porsche belonging to Lorraine Montour, sister in-law of Art Montour. She had loaned the car to an Indian male who closely resembled a wanted fugitive. The Canadian plates had expired and the Troopers issued a summons for that violation. The car was impounded in accord with the law. The following day a confrontation took place between Art Montour, Lorraine Montour and the arresting officers. Art Montour demanded the return of the auto or "White hostages would be taken along the Big Moose Road." The troopers immediately shut down the road to stop all traffic until it could be determined that the operator of the Porsche was not wanted, but the car continued to be impounded. No action to take hostages ever took place and Montour was not arrested for making the threat. Eventually, the roadway was reopened to traffic. The operator was not a wanted fugitive.

The Mohawks also claimed that the troopers were harassing them by making noise with their outside speakers as they drove by the encampment and, in one case, by using their siren and red lights. Charland explained that the keying or tapping on the mike of a troop car was meant to inform the Indians that they were passing and alert the Indian's as to who they were. In some cases the troopers could be operating C.I. (concealed identity cars), so this became a logical pattern. The use of the siren and red lights was in regard to a complaint of a White walking along the Big Moose road in the vicinity of the mountain stronghold.

The second meeting in Albany was held on February 5, 1975 and was also secret and informal. The meeting was to be chaired by Josh Stuhlburg and Thomas Colosi and the usual cast of characters. Added to the mix was another arbitrator of Rochester, New York, brought in by the National Center for Dispute Settlement (NCDS), an arm of the American Arbitration Association (AAA).

From that point on, the meetings became very secret and their locations scattered all over the state. Ogden Reid accomplished almost nothing and was finally replaced by Mario Cuomo, the Lieutenant Governor, an indication that the State was getting serious about accomplishing something. At about this time Major Robert Charland retired from the Division and went to work as the head of security at Rochester Gas and Electric. However, he continued to be a member of the State negotiation team.

For the most part, COPCA and the public, were kept in the dark as to the content of these meetings, and they, vehemently complained to the State. Then after receiving a copy of a taped speech made by the arbitrator, wherein he made disparaging remarks about COPCA and Mike Blair their spokesman, COPCA decided to make a complaint to the Governor. The interview of the arbitrator was part of the program: Ganienkeh - The Long Trail Home, made available to all radio stations in New York State.

"He said: I think the problem with COPCA in the past has been that the group was born out of lack of attention of State officials to what they consider was their problem in the prior administration in the Governor's office. It had become in my opinion, somewhat...eh... too militant and certainly not very objective at this point in time. But I would be unfair to them if I didn't point out that...eh...that without some organization the prior administartion in the Governor's office in Albany, the Wilson administration, never made any effort to talk with other people that lived in the area beside the territory of Ganienkeh, and they became frustrated and that organization and that organization was born out of that kind of thing. I don't agree with their tactics, and I totally disagree with their employment of one Michael Blair, who in my opinion is an agitator of the first order."

The typewriter in the Bennett house hit the bond paper with gusto. Doug Bennett, president of COPCA, drafted his letter of complaint to Ogden Reid, Commissioner of Conservation, asking for the dismissal of the arbitrator from the negotiation team. Then after a full discussion by COPCA, the organization decided to hold back on the letter, citing the progress made and the sensitivity needed for a successful conclusion to the negotiations. The obvious bias of the negotiator was hard to swallow, but the successful outcome of the State's efforts trumped the ouster of this man.

During the nearly three years of negotiations, the Mohawk's had been offered land on tug hill and in Jefferson and St. Lawrence Counties, but the properties were not satisfactory to their needs. They needed agriculturally sound land, with water and timber that was viable for their return to the traditional way of life they envisioned. These offers seemed to be window dressing and the negotiations continued.

It seemed that when talks would stall for some unknown reason, something of an emergency nature would occur at the Moss lake fortress. At about 2:00 a.m. one early morning the deskman at the

Romey Gallo and Wayne Martin

New Hartford station received a call from Art Montour at the Indian encampment. Montour was very excited and reported that vigilantes were burglarizing the buildings at Ganienkeh and the Indians were shooting at them. The desk man could hear gun fire in the background. Zone Sergeant Gallo, who was in charge of the zone that evening, mounted up and headed into the mountains. The post troopers were advised of the situation and told to stop and identify every user of the Big Moose Road. Gallo again used the travel time to plan how to identify the alleged perpetrator. Traveling at near one hundred miles an hour on Route 12, with red lights and siren in operation, he was quickly approaching a tractor trailer truck in front of him. The truck was in the driving lane and failed to see or hear the siren, and drifted into the passing lane as the State Police car was along side. That action by the operator of the truck forced Gallo into the separation mall of the four lane roadway, striking a warning delineator. The officer did not stop as the car seemed fine, and he continued towards Ganienkeh. His thoughts then turned to how would they, the Troopers, capture the encroacher. He remembered that there was another way into Ganienkeh by way of the Bubb Lake trail, and if he was to harass the Indians he would use that trail. It was about a three mile walk from Route 28. He made a mental note to check for any vehicle parked at that location. Traveling at break neck speed on the roadway, which was very curvy at that point, and the other thoughts going through his head, he was two miles past the parking area for the Bubb Lake Trail when he remembered his plan. After about forty five minutes of travel time, the officer turned off his emergency lighting and siren as he approached the encampment. He was met at the gate by Montour who ran to the Troop car. As he stepped from the State Police car, more gunfire rang out. The whistle of rounds overhead and clipped leaves falling around them resulted in both he and Montour scrambling to their bellies on the ground in back of the State car. Montour was holding a walkie talkie radio and Gallo said to him," for God's sake Art, tell them to stop shooting or they'll kill one another." Montour obliged and the shooting stopped. The Indians reported that, to their knowledge no one had been hurt and they had no idea who was breaking into the cabins. Of course, no investigation could be conducted by the State Police and Gallo had to wonder what the purpose of his was driving one hundred miles an hour on mountain roads, striking a delineator, only to be shot at. No vehicles had passed either State Police post during the time of the complaint.

On his return trip back to Zone Headquarters, Gallo stopped at the point where he had struck the delineator to determine the amount of damage. The delineator was only bent over as it had passed beneath the car and the officer was able to return it to its prior position. The car did not have any mechanical problems, but was checked the following day at a local garage.

With the arrival of daylight, the local patrol checked with the Indians and the medical facilities to see if any injuries had been reported. None had been, and no missing persons were reported in or near the area, so it was assumed that all was well.

The question as to whether or not the complaint was authentic remained unsolved. It should be noted that from the first call received at State Police New Hartford, until the shooting stopped upon Gallo's arrival, no less than one hour had passed. Does it seem realistic that intruders would stay in the encampment for that period of time while being exposed to continued gun fire? Or possibly the Indian's were so spooked as to continue to shoot at shadows or one another? That one would be logged as unknown, but suspicions remained high.

CHAPTER 14

TREATIES OR CONTRACTS

On November 24, 1974, after the shooting of the two whites, the Warriors put together nine previous shooting incidents that were directed at Ganienkeh by the vigilantes operating in the area. A complaint was then made to the federal government in accord with the Canandaugua Treaty of 1794. It is believed that this was done to bolster their defense for the shooting of Drake and Madigan and to shore up their side of the issue. The complaint was made by the Grand Counsel of the Iroquois Confederacy.

The following excerpts were taken from the overall complaint:

1. On July 15, 1974 at about 5:00 p.m. a United States Citizen fired shots at Ganienkeh. The 22 caliber shots were fired by a passenger of a jeep-like vehicle on the roadway a few yards from the main gate of the settlement, in direction of Indian people and houses at Ganienkeh. The State Police were called and the person subsequently arrested for possession of an illegal weapon.
2. In September, 1974 at the opening of bear season, at about 7:00 p.m. a person believed to be a United States citizen fired a high powered rifle into Ganienkeh from the Big Moose Road. The shot was fired from a blue pickup truck with a plywood camper bearing a white stripe. The shot was fired from a position near the north gate to the Indian settlement.

3. On October 20, 1974, three men, United States citizens caused a disturbance at the main gate of Ganienkeh by using abusive language towards the people of Ganienkeh, blowing the horn of their vehicle and behaving in a threatening manner. The men then left the area and proceeded across the Big Moose Road to another area of Ganienkeh. The men refused to leave when ordered. Eventually they left the area but the same vehicle returned an hour later. This time six shots were fired from the vehicle in rapid succession at the people of Ganienkeh who were on the east side of the Big Moose Road and south of the main gate. The State Police know the identity of these assailants.

4. On October 26, 1974 at about 9:00p.m. a person or persons believed to be United States citizens riding in a blue Chevrolet automobile shouted obscenities and war whoops while passing Ganienkeh going in the direction of Big Moose. The same car returned about an hour later and came to a virtual stop near the main gate to Ganienkeh. As their car stopped a rifle barrel appeared through the window of the car. Shots were fired from the car as it pulled away from the main gate.

5. On October 27, 1974 two young boys of Ganienkeh were fired upon by a person believed to be a United States Citizen. The boys sought refuge behind a rock at the back of Moss Lake and cried out, "We're here, don't shoot." Their cries were answered by war whoops and a total of about eight more shots were fired striking the ground next to the boys. This incident was reported to the State Police.

6. On October 27, just after dark, a person or persons believed to be United States Citizens riding in an automobile and coming from the direction of Big Moose fired three shots at the main gate at Ganienkeh.

7. On October 28, 1974 at about 5:15 p.m., a white Chrysler driven by a person believed a United States citizen rapidly approached Ganienkeh from Eagle Bay. As the car neared the main gate, its occupants shouted obscenities at Indians near the creek, and then quickly drove towards the north gate of Ganienkeh. At this time, one or more occupants, fired shots

at an old Indian man chopping wood, after which the car continued in the direction of Big Moose. At about 6:00 pm. The same vehicle returned, stopping near several Indians standing by the road. The driver gunned his engine and the car rapidly drove off as a shot or shots were heard from the car. The State Police and the Supervisor of the Town of Webb were immediately notified at 6:20 p.m. and no action was taken to prevent the subsequent shootings from the car as it passed the main gate. The State Police then arrived at 8:45 p.m.
8. On October 29,1974, at about 6:30 p.m., a person believed to be a United States Citizen riding in an automobile coming from the direction of Big Moose fired a small caliber weapon into Ganienkeh near the north gate. As the automobile approached the main gate to Ganienkeh it slowed down. Small caliber shots and a high powered shot were heard from the car as it passed the main gate. The State Police then arrived at 8:45 p.m.
9. On Nov 6, 1974 at about 9:00 a.m. two shots were fired by a person or persons believed to be United States Citizens at Moss Lake in proximity to the dwelling houses of Ganienkeh.
10. On the same day at about 11:30 a.m. five shots were fired by a person or persons believed to be United State Citizens in proximity of adults and children washing clothes at Moss Lake.

The complaint to President Ford does not indicate, every time harassment occurred, that the Indians reported the same to the State Police. When notified, the Troopers always tried to investigate as best they could, without being allowed inside Ganienkeh and without the opportunity to interview witnesses.

On November 24, 1974 the United States lodged a formal complaint of their own with the Chiefs of the Six Nation Iroquois Confederacy. The Commissioner of Indian Affairs, Morris Thompson, directed a letter to the confederacy with regard to the shooting incident of Aprile Madigan and Stephen Drake by the Indians. By lodging the complaint, the U.S. government complied with article VII of the Treaty of 1794, which states that matters of this nature are to be worked out between the President of the U.S. and the Mohawk Nation. This elated the Indians, adding the much needed acceptance of the treaty by the government and giving muscle to their sovereignty issue. The Commissioner's letter to President Ford does not indicate that each and every time harassment occurred that the Indians reported the same to the State Police. When notified, the Troopers always tried to investigate as best they could, without being allowed inside Ganienkeh and without the opportunity to interview witnesses. According to State Police, no Indians were ever injured during these alleged encounters. Also, the guard house and meeting building did not show any marks of gunfire. This would make one believe that the shots were fired into the air and/or were fire crackers. The recommendation was that the State should continue to investigate the shooting matter with representatives of the Iroquois Confederacy.

The position of the Warrior Society and their reply to the United States was that they, the Indians, would exercise their own authority to investigate the matter with representatives from the Grand Council participating. If that was not agreeable to the United States, then the two parties should meet and decide a suitable course of action.

In a Ganienkeh news letter dated November 26, 1974 the following paragraph appeared: "The United States has taken a welcome and historic step in applying the provisions of the 1794 treaty in regard to the shooting incidents."

Shortly thereafter, the position of the U.S. Government changed, referring to the 1794 treaty, giving Congress the authority to make other equitable provisions for keeping the peace. According to the Department of Interior, "Subsequent Federal statutes confer jurisdiction on the courts of the State of New York in criminal matters arising on the reservation." But the Ganienkeh stronghold was not a reservation and the Mohawks were quick to point that fact out. The Mohawks also contended that a Treaty is a Federal contract and a contract can only be changed by the parties named thereon. How then could the Federal government confer jurisdiction on the State of New York?

Bureau of Indian Affairs (BIA) spokesman Robert Farring said, "An Indian treaty is no more than a federal law and any subsequent law passed can take precedent over that treaty." The Mohawk Indians did not agree with his interpretation and continued to contend that a Treaty is a contract and can only be changed by the agreement of both parties. It should be further noted that the U.S. Constitution forbids States from negotiating with a foreign power, and the Mohawks considered themselves sovereign at that time in history.

It seems that the Federal government realized that they were heading into a trap by almost recognizing Ganienkeh as sovereign. The government had to quickly back off and attempt to show that changes in the law allowed the Indians to negotiate and work with the State. The Mohawks at Ganienkeh did not agree that they could negotiate with the State, and by delineating their own complaints (treaty of 1794) they strengthened their defense to the shooting of Madigan and Drake and held fast to their interpretation of "What is a treaty." Most important was their reasoning for not allowing a State Police Investigation on their sovereign land.

Chapter 15

Embarrassed District Attorney

When it became obvious that the State politicians would not permit the Troopers to evict the Mohawks, and when they publicly announced that they had no intentions of removing the encroachers, the local people began to wonder what the District Attorney's role should be in this whole matter. Members of COPCA and other local residents began to apply pressure on Henry Blumberg, the District Attorney of Herkimer County, to take some action. In addition, Senator Donovan and Assemblyman William Sears also began to ask the same question, and they let Blumberg know how they felt: It was time for a lot less political talk and a lot more action by the District Attorney.

Blumberg, the D.A., had been elected to office several times in the county and was well thought of. He had also worked very closely with the State Police and had an excellent rapport with them. He also had a large ego, and when the pressure began to mount, he decided to take some legal action of his own, and meant, of course, to cover his behind. He appeared before Town Justice Sam Herman, Town of Webb Justice Court, and filed an affidavit for a search warrant of Ganienkeh in an effort to recover the weapons used to shoot and injure Drake and Madigan. The Troopers had recovered the projectiles that caused the injuries and perhaps would be able to match the weapons to the armor piercing rounds at the State Police Laboratory in Albany, by using the lands and groove method of identification. When a barrel of a weapon is bored out it starts as a smooth bore. The grooves are cut out in a spiral form leaving the lands as the raised areas between each groove. This is called rifling, and causes different markings in every firearm. These markings leave their own telltale print on each projectile fired. They are the fingerprint of the weapon.

The search warrant was turned over to the Troopers for execution and immediately came under scrutiny by the officers. The warrant called for the search of the entire six hundred and twelve acres of Ganienkeh in an effort to confiscate the wanted weapons. From the onset, the Troopers knew that a search warrant could not be that large in scope, but must be quite specific regarding what should be searched. The matter was turned over to the Attorney General of the State who agreed with the State Police that the warrant would indeed be illegal. Major Charland then reminded Blumberg that it would take three hundred Troopers to execute such a warrant. The District Attorney, now knowing that the Troopers were right and that they would not go along with the flawed warrant, realized its' execution would bring about the bloodbath the Troopers were attempting to avoid. The D.A. quietly let the matter drift off into the sunset.

But Blumberg was not finished. In August of 1975, he obtained a subpoena for the leaders of Ganienkeh to appear before him on the matter of the land dispute. At that time, the Mohawk Warrior Society had already ignored the jurisdiction of the State Courts and made a mockery of the State's judicial system. A plain clothes Deputy Sheriff attempted to serve the subpoena on the Indians and told the Warriors they were trespassing on State land. The braves refused to accept the piece of paper. They advised him, "You are the trespasser" and ordered him to leave. The deputy laid the subpoena on a log by the gate and turned to leave. The Indians quickly advised him that he was littering and told him to pick up his papers. The deputy complied and quickly left the Moss Lake area. Later, Blumberg attempted to serve the subpoena by mail. The Warriors expected this move and when the registered mail arrived, they refused to accept it and sent it back to the District Attorney. Blumberg continued his quest, and when the Indians failed to appear before him to answer questions concerning the land takeover, he told the press that he would seek a default judgment against them. He stated that the default judgment, if obtained, would declare the State the lawful owner of Ganienkeh. The District Attorney stated that he would seek action from a county Grand Jury to obtain a trespass violation against the Mohawks.

At a later time, Chief Robert Crofoot, Town of Webb PD, who was liked by the Indians, was able to serve a subpoena on the Mohawks with regard to their appearance before the County Court. Although they accepted the subpoena they never appeared as directed. After a considerable amount of time had elapsed, and the Mohawks failed to appear, he declared that the matter was a Federal issue and could not be decided by the State. His challenger for the upcoming election in the fall of 1975, Martin Weinstein, used Blumberg's failure to exercise his sworn duties and remove the Warriors when they first occupied the Moss Lake land as a reason for his removal from office. Blumberg quickly turned to the Federal issue to answer Weinstein's accusation. He was re-elected to his position of District Attorney of Herkimer County.

Frustrated by the Warrior Society, Blumberg stepped quietly back out of the foray, knowing that he had at least used all of his weapons. With the knowledge that State and Federal courts would not help, he resigned himself to the background. It certainly seemed that the Warrior Society was winning all the legal battles.

Chesebro Commended in Moss Lake Affair

by John Isley

"The round out," "the opportunity for a trooper to discuss function and the development of insight and the workings of the Indian and the white man." The words of a 22-year veteran of the New York State Police and his involvement in the Moss Lake Indian dispute. Trooper William F. Chesebro now assigned as station commander of the Old Forge sub-station has had the opportunity to have first hand experience in the day to day developments of the armed Indian takeover of the 612 acre girls camp in the Adirondacks at Moss Lake near Eagle Bay in Herkimer County.

Chesebro has now received three letters commending him for his outstanding duty during the last four years of the Indian takeover. Chesebro said he was assigned to Old Forge station, then under Trooper A.J. Smith now retired, the day of the Indian takeover to "beef up the Old Forge patrol." Chesebro became active in the full investigation of the problem on Oct. 28, 1974 when the shooting of two whites near the Indian encampment occurred. He was on vacation at that time, but reported to the Eagle Bay fire station, when the shots were fired that injured Steven Drake of Inlet. Since Sept. of 1975 Chesebro was under full orders of now retired Maj. Robert Charland of Troop D to act as a liason between the whites and Indians at Moss Lake.

This action did not come from the request of the some 50 white families living in the Big Moose area, but the Indians requested Chesebro. Chesebro noted that the American Indian has "gained a distrust for any enforcement officer." Chesebro had been building what he described as "fairness and creditibility" with the Indians and the whites since the 1974 shootings.

The Indians charges of whites shooting at the Indian encampment were not always unfounded. Chesebro said he knew of at least three times when the Indian claims were founded...he was not sure if the Indians had fired weapons in those incidents. Chesebro remained cautious during the interview stating that Moss Lake was still an "ongoing investigation" by the State Police.

"Moss Lake is not over," Chesebro said, "as long as there is an occupancy there is a problem." The state is allowing the Indians to stay at Moss Lake until July 1, 1978 to remove buildings from the site to their new location in Clinton County. The location in Altona was given to the Indians by the state following the closing of negotiations between the two on May 13, 1977. Chesebro believes the Indians will leave July 1.

The "ongoing Indian takeover and actions are patterns now being set by minority groups," Chesebro explained. Looking back into the dispute and negotiations Chesebro said, "If you knew Wednesday what you knew on Friday," sometimes you would have done things a little differently.

The Moss Lake syndrome is not over either. Chesebro said that other Indian land takeovers will occur and mentioned the recent land claim by the Oneidas and the possible closing of the Thousand Islands on April 1, by Indians there.

The agreement that concluded a armed takeover of Moss Lake has set a precedent, Chesebro said. The package presented to the Indians by Secretary of State Mario Cuomo was the same as presented by former Department of Environmental Conservation Commissioner Ogden Reid. Reid put the "foot in the door," but Reid ran into political problems with Gov. Carey and resigned from the job before the Moss Lake negotiations were over.

The several million dollars spent by state taxpayers for State Police protection at Moss Lake was "necessary," Chesebro said. Moss Lake has been defused however, the trooper believes. When you reduce the number of participants in any issue you have defused it, Chesebro said.

Quoting from the Letters of Commendation Chesebro received, the words of Dr. Joseph Stulberg from the American Arbitration Association, "Bill spent many days and months working in close collaboration with our on-site intern Scott Buchheit. On many occasions, what other circumstances would have been normal arguments between neighbors turned into almost violent confrontations. The professional decorum and maturity displayed by Bill in these situations prevented all of them from escalating into unfortunate and regrettable instances in which people were harmed."

Maj. Robert Charland said of Chesebro, "'your police knowledge and expert woodsmanship were invaluable during the prolonged murder investigation of Bernard Hatch and your presence at Old Forge has been one of the most stabilizing factors in the Moss Lake situation.

Chesebro served under several Majors during the Moss Lake problem and the words of the last Major were...and we quote from retired Major William F. Keefe. "This knowledge and rapport has been invaluable to the State Police especially to Major Robert Charland and myself and to New York Secretary of State Mario Cuomo. I want you to know that your efforts are recognized and appreciated as a result you have gained the respect of the Indians, the American Arbitration Association, the Secretary of State and myself."

Chesebro joined the New York State Police on June 21, 1956 and has served in what he termed as "all phases" of the state police in troops A, D, F & T. His duties have ranged from Communications, Thruway photographer and marksman.

Some of the problems faced by Chesebro during the last four years included "representing rank," a trooper serving in the position of an officer. Chesebro said that he didn't always agree with the position, but the position was presented.

State Police continue daily routine checks of Moss Lake, but the full uniform protection has left the area. The number of complaints continue from both sides, but they too have declined.

When Chesebro was asked "why the Indian takeover occured in the Adirondacks he said that because it was the Mohawk land, the land of the Flint...but because like the mountain climber....it was here."

When joining the New York State Police 22 years ago, the young trooper never thought that he would become a major part of an Indian takeover that can be compared only next to "Wounded Knee"...but due to the actions of a trooper named William Chesebro, the outcome was different. If Chesebro hadn't been there he said he might not have believed it.

TROOPER WILLIAM F. CHESEBRO from the Old Forge State Police has received several letters commending him for his outstanding effort during the Moss Lake Indian takeover. (Photo by John Isley)

Chapter 16

Threats Firearms & Firewater

It seemed to the State Police that tensions were escalating over Ganienkeh. Things had cooled between the parties involved after the shootings, but were now on the rise once again. During the first week of January, 1976, COPCA received a copy of a letter allegedly written by Louis Hall, Secretary of the Ganienkeh Council fire, to a gun dealer on Long Island. The letter asked about the possibility of the dealer supplying the Indians with twenty Armlite AR-15 assault rifles and 20,000 rounds of ammunition for the guns. Hall, allegedly asked for a quote, and a means of delivery, if the guns were available. Hall's signature was on the letter, which the Warriors said was a forgery. It was post marked Eagle Bay, NY, Nov 17, 1975. The opened letter had been mailed to COPCA from the Akwesasne Reservation.

A comparison of the signature on the letter with one that was known to be Louis Hall's was made by the State Police Laboratory in Albany. The differences were obvious and the letter appeared to be a forgery. However, a letter of that seriousness could be written and the signature disguised, by having an associate sign the author's name. It would certainly appear that it was a forgery, in that it indeed was not the author's signature. The Indians at that time had all the weapons they could ever ask for. It didn't seem they needed more guns or would risk purchasing any while negotiations were underway. It should be noted that firearms from this particular dealer had ended up in the Middle East in the past. The mystery of who at Akwesasne disliked the Warriors enough to perpetrate the fraud became the question. It goes without saying, that the gun dealer on Long Island certainly would not have given anyone a copy of such a letter, one indicating that he dealt with illegal guns. The Mohawks at Akwesasne had not approved of the Warriors' takeover of the Moss Lake Girls' Camp and some may have become jealous of the progress the negotiations were taking with the State and what the Warrior Society had accomplished. Perhaps, someone wished to throw a monkey wrench in the whole affair, upsetting what had been accomplished thus far by the Indians.

In the following months several incidents took place that made the State Police wonder if Chief Louis Hall, Art Montour and other elders were losing control of the younger braves. If that happened a crisis of a grave nature could occur, perhaps another Wounded Knee.

On June 30, 1976, State Police received reliable information that a group of radical Indians were coming down from Hogansburg (Akwesasne) to "ambush" a Trooper. The informant mentioned the names of several Troopers as well as "any cop." The threatened Troopers were individually advised and Major Charland, who was in Washington at the time, was called and informed of the threat. Trooper details also were advised of the information and were instructed to use extreme caution.

On July 4th, two White males reported that Indians at Ganienkeh pointed rifles at them as they passed the encampment in their car, and they had done nothing to provoke the Warriors. Incidents of this nature seemed to be building.

Shortly thereafter, a local informant notified Troopers of a red Cadillac, new to the area, occupied by four Indians. The vehicle was stopped at outpost one and the occupants identified as Stoney, White Feather,"FaFa", and an Indian female "Ginny." After a thorough search of the Cadillac, the Indians were allowed to proceed to Ganienkeh. Obviously, the Troopers were stepping up their enforcement efforts, despite the absence of orders to do so by Zone Headquarters or Troop.

On July 15, 1976, off duty Trooper Don Kirkpatrick, stopped at the Mountain Side Inn, Inlet, for a sandwich and a beer. The owner recognized Kirkpatrick as a Trooper and quietly advised him of another patron in the bar (an Indian) who had been trying to sell him what he believed to be a fully automatic weapon. A fully automatic weapon continues to shoot in rapid succession when the trigger is pulled and held back, as opposed to a semi automatic that fires one shot each time the trigger is activated. The off duty Trooper asked the owner to purchase the weapon so that it could be inspected by the State Police and agents from the Alcohol, Tobacco and Firearms (A.T.F.) to ensure that it violated the law, before they took steps to arrest the Indian. The proprietor purchased the weapon from "Stony" for one hundred dollars. When Stony left the bar, the weapon was identified as a "Bushmaster Machine Pistol" 5.56 caliber. The serial number had been filed off which made it impossible to determined at that time if the weapon was "hot" (stolen or used in a crime). Trooper Kirkpatrick then called Zone Headquarters at New Hartford to report the matter, and, additionally advised that the Indian had been talking about a fifty caliber machine gun set up at Ganienkeh. Because of previous threats to ambush a Trooper, and the fear the elders were losing control of the Mountain Stronghold, Zone Sergeant Gallo and Sgt. Julian responded from zone headquarters, picking up Trooper Chesebro, who was off duty, on the way.

As they exited the Troop car at the Mountainside Inn, a coyote could be heard howling a mile or so away in the mountains. This added to the intrigue of the night. The trio of officers went inside to meet with Trooper Kirkpatrick. It was about 10:00 p.m. when a phone call was received from a confidential informant that something out of the ordinary was about to occur. The information was vague but led to the belief that it could be an attempt by the Warriors to regain possession of the weapon and to get Stony back at the encampment before further damage could be done. A Trooper from the Old Forge Station was posted outside the Inn in a wooded area, and the curtains on all the windows of the Inn were drawn, and the doors locked. Two shotguns were taken inside for additional fire power, should it be needed. Shortly thereafter, the officers were joined by Captain Loomis, the acting Troop Commander. Gallo felt the anxiety and stress mount and wondered if the other officers felt the same. By their mannerisms, it appeared that they too were feeling the pressure of what might happen. These Indians had proven that they were capable of almost anything. They had already shot two people and anything of a radical nature could be expected. After approximately one hour of discussion, and preparation concerning the new information and the threats, the Troopers turned to the Bushmaster and confiscated the weapon, believing it to be fully automatic. The owner of the lodge elaborated on his talk with Stony regarding the fifty caliber machine gun being brought into the stronghold and set up to cover the front gate. The question then became, "What were the warriors planning to do with the fifty caliber weapon?" Perhaps it was going to be used for some purpose other than covering the front gate. How many more weapons of that nature were inside the encampment? Had the young braves assumed control of the Warrior's activities? The Troopers anxiously waited for more information from their informant, but none came. It was now early morning and nothing of an unusual nature had occurred. In addition to the Old Forge patrol and the fixed posts, two extra Troopers stayed in the area in the event of some overt act by the Mohawks, with particular attention given to the Mountain Side Inn, albeit without the knowledge of Stony.

While on duty the following day, Trooper Kirkpatrick observed Stony hitchhiking (a violation) on Route 28 and arrested him for the minor offense, taking him to the Old Forge State Police Station at the direction of Zone Sergeant Gallo. At 7:40 a.m., Trooper Chesebro arrived and interviewed the suspect. He was identified as Stone Hawk Goeman of the Seneca Nation. He had been working at the Minnow Brook Motel while staying at Ganienkeh. He had recently been excommunicated from the Indian stronghold for drinking and was living at the Mountain Lodge. Senior Investigator Gildersleeve arrived at the station and continued to interview Stony. He denied that the Indians at Ganienkeh had a fifty caliber machine gun, stating "That was only beer talk." He did, however, outline all of the smaller caliber weapons, including two AR-15 fully automatic weapons, further stating that everyone at Ganienkeh was armed with rifles and shotguns, even some of the women. He also claimed there were ten cases of dynamite buried at the Indian encampment, although he could not give, or perhaps did not want to give, the location of the underground magazine. It had been some time since he was an occupant of Ganienkeh and was unable to assess the current feelings between the younger braves and their leaders, which was of the utmost importance to the Troopers.

Trooper Chesebro took a written statement from the owner of the Mountainside, regarding the weapon, and from whom he purchased it.

Stone Hawk was arraigned in the Town of Webb Justice Court on the charge of "hitchhiking," to which he pled guilty. He was then taken to New Hartford to meet with the F.B.I. and the A.T.F. to ascertain if he had committed any federal violations.

While at the court, Trooper Chesebro talked to "White Feather," identified as Eugene Robert Cameron, a friend of Stone Hawk. The Indian bragged of being set free after shooting a federal agent in the hand when he was fourteen years old. He had lived in Massachusetts and in Canada before coming to Moss Lake. He was not wanted anywhere, but Chesebro had to wonder if he was sent there to be the assassin of a State Trooper. The entire Trooper details, the DEC, and Town of Webb PD, were notified of this possibility.

The arrest of Stone Hawk and the previous threats against State Police energized the whole investigation and brought out the Troopers' brass; acting Troop Commander Loomis and Lieutenant Pete Goodwin arrived in Old Forge after the arrest of Stone Hawk.

When Art Montour learned of the arrest of Stony Goeman from Scott Buckheit, he requested a meeting with State Police, which he got. Because the Old Forge Station is so small, the meeting was held outside on a picnic table. The following subjects were present: Loomis, Goodwin, Chesebro, Montour, another unidentified Indian male and Scott Buckhiet of the (AAA). The officers confronted Montour with the information that Stony had provided, with regard to the fifty caliber machine gun, the other fully automatic weapons and the dynamite. Montour denied the existence of all the weapons that Stone Hawk described and became very angry. He said, "Someone is lying" and "Stone Hawk should be committed." He readily admitted that he previously saw the Bushmaster that Stony had sold and stated that it would only fire one shot at a time. It turned out that Montour was correct concerning the weapon. It was not a violation except for the filed down serial number.

The Troopers sent the "Bushmaster" to the State Police Laboratory in Albany in an effort to raise the serial numbers. The technique did not work and they could not determine if the weapon was hot. The possession of a weapon with filed down serial numbers was a violation of New York State law and Goeman was charged with a crime, fingerprinted, and photographed. He pled guilty and was fined $200.00.

The Troopers took him back to the Mountain Side Inn where he had lived and left him there. Later, he found his way back to Ganienkeh, most likely taken there by the Indians, where he had to face the wrath of the Mohawk leaders. Scott Buckheit (AAA) confirmed that Stoney was in fact, back at the camp about a week later.

Montour complained to the Troopers that Stoney had been interrogated concerning the best access into the Indian encampment for a State Police assault and other secret matters, (number of Braves, booby traps, etc). Apparently this line of questioning brought back the threat of a forceful State eviction (which the DEC had promised would not occur), rekindling the Indian's fear. Montour believed the State Police were out of line questioning an Indian who was part of Ganienkeh. This went to show how far the Indians believed their immunity should be recognized. Of course, Montour was very wrong in his belief and the Troopers quickly enlightened him.

Two days after the arrest of Stone Hawk Goeman, Trooper Kirkpatrick was reassigned out of the area. This was done by the Zone Office in an effort to protect him from a possible attempt on his life. He was not one of the Troopers mentioned in the threats received, but, after the arrest of Stone Hawk, he could have been a marked Trooper. For the time being, things had cooled considerably.

CHAPTER 17

A WHITE KNUCKLE NIGHT

Webster's Dictionary defines the term Indian Giver as a person who gives something and then takes it back, from the belief that American Indians expected an equivalent in return when giving something. If the Indians felt that the trade was not equal or better they would renig on the deal. Actually this was the way of their barter. It appears to be a legitimate way of doing business and an unfair stereotype of the Native American. A second definition stems from the practice of the White Man and his inability to abide by his contracts with the Indians. Many historians now agree, that when it came to honesty, the Native Americans were far out front of the Europeans. The Indians of today call the 1600's landing of the pilgrims a bad day for the Redman. From that time forward, their land was slowly taken from them by the pilgrims. They were pushed onto reservations and entered into treaties with the encroachers. But in many cases, when the land given to the Indian became valuable (minerals or needed space) the treaties were broken and the land taken back for the use of the Whites. In many circles this type of action also has been known as the possible definition of Indian Giver.

A third definition of this idiom is presented by the authors of this book: the introduction of Indian Giving for another purpose. The State of New York in a series of giving's to the Mohawks to settle the Indian occupation of the Moss Lake Girls Camp, have created their own definition of Indian Giving, giving in to every whim of the Mohawks in an effort to appease them. However, this action by the State, which appears to be very liberal in nature, has been used by the State to beef up local economies by relocating the Indians to the area most needing a shot in the arm. Casinos and bingo halls seem to be par for the course when individual Indian Nations are relocated and are encouraged by the State.

In July 1975, the Department of Environmental Conservation gave birth to another major piece of Indian Giving by the State (Sovereignty and Symbol - Landsman 1988). The first major piece of "Indian Giving" was of course the State's election not to defend Moss Lake, allowing the Indian occupation in the first place. This new piece of Indian Giving occurred when the Moss Lake area, held by the Indians, was declared a "defacto" reservation by the Conservation Commissioner, Ogden Reid. This led to the creation of an artificial boundary line that encompassed Moss Lake, Bubb Lake, and Sis Lake, thus adding to the Mohawks newly acclaimed sovereign nation, nearly tenfold to the original 612 acres. This artificial line was very loosely described and no one knew exactly where it was. The environmental laws within this area would be suspended with regard to the Native Americans. Although not specifically addressed, the Indians took the immunity a step further, something they later took advantage of by exempting themselves from all laws within that area. An example of this was their indiscriminate cutting of logs within this added area, and on private and other State land adjacent thereto. The Troopers and Forest Rangers failure to file charges for these acts of larceny, in effect, gave the Mohawks tacit approval in the belief that no law was to be enforced against them, on or near Ganienkeh. This act by the Commissioner was legal. He did have the right to suspend the ENCON laws, but no others. This action implied that no laws could be enforced against the Indians within that area (the sovereign nation). In other words, the Mohawks continued with the belief that neither the State of New York, nor the Federal Government had jurisdiction over them. The Troopers and other officers knew that it was, hands off, when it came to the Warrior Society.

An additional error by DEC officials was their failure to confer with the State Police on this matter. This action allowed the age old problem of jealousy amongst departments to rear its ugly head. After all, the Troopers were charged with enforcing all the laws in the area and were doing ninety nine percent of the police work and knew all that was known about the situation. Also there was no evidence of DEC officials discussing the matter with their own men in the field. The men in the trenches were the ones who would know the merits of the plan, not someone sitting behind a desk in Albany. When part time employee Barny Barnum of the DEC was asked as to whether the men in the field had any input, he stated, "are you kidding." The complete impunity given to the Mohawks was not publicized, and if it had been, the information would have only added to the anger already present amongst the white community.

This action by the Commissioner of DEC, and prepared by Senior Counsel, Martin Wasser, was met with criticism and sarcasm by the employees of the Department. It was referred to as, "The Marty Wasser Keep Out Edict." State Troopers, who were also charged with enforcement of the DEC laws, took exception to its existence, as they had never had to deal with police matters with their hands completely tied, except the handling of foreign diplomats. Most officers could foresee future problems. Why was it done and who was behind it? This is another burning question that has been impossible to trace down. It didn't seem that it would have a positive impact on the Indian/White relationship. In fact, many felt that the more area given to the Mohawks could mean more adversarial contacts between the Whites and the Indians, not less. This move by the DEC became another negative mark against the State and another point of aggravation for COPCA, who now saw it as another act of liberal politicians giving away State land, and giving in to every whim of the Mohawk Warrior Society.

The edict, as it became known, flew in the face of most of the dedicated officers. If a serious crime was now committed within the defacto reservation, or close thereto, a question of jurisdiction could easily arise from either side, making a nose to nose confrontation a reality. This newly sanctioned ground could become covered with blood and an escalation of the conflict would closely follow. To most officers, this was a travesty. A few, could see some merit to this decision, if it somehow kept the Troopers, the Whites and Indians apart. It couldn't, more territory meant more contact between Whites and the Indians that the Whites were use to using. It did assist the Indians by providing a greater food source, as their hunting area was greatly enlarged. Overall, it indeed was another "Indian Giving" by New York State, a rose for the Indians and another thorn in the side of the people of the State. It seemed that everything was done to benefit the encroachers and the Troopers predicted it would lead to more difficulty for the future. The officers were right in this regard, as this enlarged territory nearly cost a Trooper or Troopers their lives.

On Dec 10, 1975 the fears of the State Troopers became a reality. Trooper Tom Kelly, a seasoned officer, was manning the northern checkpoint when he was told by a passing motorist that several Indians were carrying a deer down the Big Moose Road towards Ganienkeh. The trooper secured his post and advised the New Hartford zone station by radio of the situation, receiving permission to leave his post. While en route to the scene, Kelly couldn't help but wonder why the Indians would bring the deer down the Big Moose Road when there was any number of trails through the woods that would lead to the Mohawks encampment. In the back of his mind he wondered if this was a scripted encounter. The Trooper caught up to the Indians about one half mile north of the encampment.

Most people have seen pictures of Indian hunters carrying their big game back to their people on a pole, and Trooper Kelly saw just that as he arrived on the scene. Four young Indian males had what Kelly described as a freshly killed doe deer tied by its feet to each end of an eight foot pole, hanging upside down, with the ends of the pole resting on the shoulders of the two young carriers. It must be noted that Kelly had to be cognizant of everything going on around him, and that was a lot. It was early evening and darkness was closing in. Kelly exited his vehicle armed only with his 357 magnum, leaving the 12 gauge Ithaca shotgun behind. It wasn't necessary for him to pull the revolver from its holster as the young Indians seemed cooperative and not aggressive. Being a very mild mannered officer, Kelly quickly established a rapport with the Warriors. While he assessed the situation and looked for signs of entrapment, he realized that he could be the target of an assassinations attempt. The last thing he wanted to do was agitate the situation if he didn't need to. He also realized that if he made an arrest or issued an appearance ticket, the lid could come off the pot.

The young Indians alleged that they had taken the deer legally inside their defacto territory and were still in it and should not be held any longer. Were they now on Mohawk territory? Was this section of the Big Moose Road part of Ganienkeh? Where was the deer shot? Was season open? Did

Indian Givers

the Indians need a license? Did they need a tag? Was it legal to shoot a female deer in that area? These issues confronted the Trooper as he waited for orders from Troop Headquarters. Kelly took each rifle that the Indians were carrying and file checked them via radio using the serial numbers for identification. All were clean (not stolen or used in a crime). This action by Kelly was quite brave in light of his thoughts of a possible assassination attempt. What would have happened if one of the guns were hot? The trooper, being occupied with the four young Indians, did not notice that other braves had encircled him, standing behind the trees and large rocks. His concentration was on the braves that were on the roadway and beside him. Barny Barnum, a part time employee of the Department of Environmental Conservation, arrived at the scene to assist. He had learned of the conflict from his police monitor and quickly responded. Barnum observed one thing different than Kelly. He noted the stiffness of the deer and the nature of its eyes. Barnum stated, "It looked like the deer was shot a day or two before the encounter with Trooper Kelly."

Sergeant Bruce Payne, a State Policeman of 15 years, a retired naval officer, and now a no nonsense Trooper, happened to be traveling towards the Moss Lake area for a supervisory visit when he learned of Kelly's predicament. It was difficult to drive very fast on the Big Moose Road because of bumps and curves, but Payne made excellent time. As he approached the Mohawk encampment, he increased his speed. He was very much aware of the two bunkers (pill boxes) guarding the front gate of Ganienkeh. Knowing they would be manned by warriors with fully automatic weapons, Payne wasted no time speeding by. He did not wish to be in the cross hairs of an AK-14. As he broke the hill crest in front of the bunkers and the Ganienkeh gate, four of the Warriors were hastily towing a wooden wagon across the roadway, attempting to block it. The sergeant drove around the wagon, onto the shoulder and into the ditch. The whole Mohawk Nation could not have stopped him at that point as he continued north to assist Kelly. The Indians act of blocking the road was an obvious attempt at keeping further assistance out, and, if an arrest was made, an attempt at not allowing the Troopers back through with any Mohawk prisoners. And Payne knew it. The only alternative would be to take the prisoners in the opposite direction by the dirt roads that led to Still Water Landing: Probably a two hour venture over very bad roads. Upon his arrival, he and Kelly, after privately discussing the situation, would do exactly that if they made an arrest. While continuing their investigation, they pondered their situation further and formulated a plan.

Trooper Bill Chesebro, who was off duty, but in the area for a meeting with the Indians and Scott Buckheit of the American Arbitration Association, along with Arthur Montour, Ganienkeh spokesman and leader, arrived to hopefully defuse a situation that grew more tense each moment. Chesebro could see armed Indians in the shadows standing behind the trees. His estimate was seven or eight additional warriors that suddenly appeared. Darkness was upon them, but the Troopers eyes were adjusting to the change. Buckheit quickly left the scene as requested by Chesebro, to speak with Major Charland via phone. Montour, standing next to Chesebro, quietly told the Trooper that if an arrest was made there would be a shooting. Chesebro always carried a Derringer when off duty and his mind went in overdrive. He carried the weapon in his glove so that it would not be seen and quickly pushed the weapon that was inside the glove into Montour's ribs in plain sight of the braves. He knew that the Warriors would recognize what he was doing and felt this would deter any action by the young Indians, should Payne and Kelly decide to go through with the arrest. He and Montour had become friends and this action was hard for him to do. He hoped that the Indian spokesman would understand.

The scene grew very quiet and the officers there were unable to see the facial expressions of the Warriors in the darkness in order to assess their reaction to Chesebro's overt act. After what seemed like an eternity, orders came from the Troop Commander, Robert Charland, to release the young Indians with no further action taken. From Kelly's first encounter with the young warriors, only one hour had passed. Although the Trooper said afterwards, "It seemed like forever." The Troopers returned the weapons and deer to the young Indians.

It was a "White knuckle night" exclaimed a confidential informant when discussing the matter with Dr. Gail Landsman in 1978, while she was gathering information for her book. (Sovereignty and Symbol, Landsman 1988.)

A review of Trooper Chesebro's memorandum concerning this encounter revealed that he too believed the deer was shot a day or two before, lending suspicion to the possibility that this could have been a setup by the Mohawks. Additionally, why didn't the young Indians use other trails leading to the encampment, and why did the young Indians use the Big Moose Road, unless they wanted to be seen?

Threats and information received earlier indicated the possible assassination attempt of a State Trooper. Many officers felt that this was a setup was for that purpose. Some felt that if it was a setup, it was for more press and additional stirring of the pot. If it was to keep things agitated in the area, it was a very dangerous way to proceed, putting more pressure on the State to resolve the situation with more meaningful negotiations. If it was a setup to ambush a trooper, which seems more likely, then Chesebro's action and the subsequent decision by Charland not to arrest, were both on the money, keeping Kelly, Payne and Barnum alive to talk about it over a cold beer. Perhaps it kept one, or all three, from being six feet under and ten toes up.

Approximately a week later, Trooper Chesebro was invited to appear in front of the Chiefs of the Six Nations. On that day a meeting was held between the Indians and Mario Cuomo in Cicero, New York. On that day Chesebro became an honorary Warrior of the Mohawk Warrior Society for his actions to prevent a possible shooting of a New York State Trooper. Additionally, he was given the right to "speak in council" with the Chiefs in the future. This action by the Mohawk Chiefs, spells out with almost certainty, what was planned by some of the Warriors on that day. Today, Bill Chesebro always carries his Warriors membership card and is highly respected by the Mohawks.

This event also made another matter perfectly clear. Montour and the other leaders of the Warriors could not control what the younger braves wanted to do on that evening. They were losing control, and, perhaps at that time, control had already eroded to a point of grave danger. Any complacency that had crept into the trooper ranks was now foremost in the minds of all supervisors and it required a jacking up of all personnel that had to work the area. Knowing most Troopers of those times, this made their work there more exciting and invigorated the whole assignment. Complacency and boredom was not the way of life of a Trooper sworn to protect and serve. He wasn't there to get a paycheck. He was there to be a cop.

Chapter 18

The Hot Potatoes

On February 10, 1975 the lawsuit brought by the State of New York against the Mohawk Indians was heard in the Federal Court of Judge Edmond Port, Syracuse, New York. This was an attempt to get the court to hand down a judgment against the Indians that the land in question was part and parcel of the State of New York and the Mohawks had no claim to it. This suit was filed in September 1974, prior to the shooting incidents of the Whites, and previously described.

From the beginning, upon their arrival at Moss Lake, the Mohawks claimed sovereignty and made it known that they would not negotiate with the State, nor federal governments, and would not acknowledge their laws or courts. Citing the 1794 treaty of Canandaigua between the United States and the Iroquois Nation, they were compelled to settle any difference only with the President of the United States, Gerald Ford.

The Indians appeared with their attorney's Tim Coulter and Nancy Stearns, associates of the radical civil rights lawyer William Kunstler, best known for his involvement in the Wounded Knee Insurrection of 1973. The state was represented by attorney general Jeremiah Jochnowitz. The Mohawks quickly let it be known that their appearance was not meant to litigate the land matter but only to plead their case that the court had no jurisdiction over them and that the land matter must be handled by the mandates of the 1794 treaty. According to the attorneys for the Indians, it would be totally improper for the court to sit in judgment between two nations, the U.S. and the Mohawk Indians.

The judge gave the Indians twenty days to answer the briefs submitted by the state, the property owners and the Town of Webb. The Attorney General made a motion for a summary judgment which was denied by the court. The Indians countered with their own motion to dismiss because of the lack of jurisdiction. This was also denied at that time by the court.

The attorneys for the Indians in a very up front fashion advised the judge that they would not submit to the jurisdiction of the court. It was reported that the Judge was visibly upset with this development, but the Indians stuck to their guns, and from that time forward, they would only talk about jurisdiction. Art Montour stated that they, the Mohawks, would no longer appear in the court. The attorney's would answer the jurisdictional briefs in writing and then the Mohawks would be done. The Mohawks had defied the rule of law of the United States and the State of New York. If a member of COPCA or any non-Indian had defied the U.S. Court they no doubt would be held in contempt and, most likely, jailed.

Eventually, Judge Port did dismiss the action because of his lack of jurisdiction and remanded the case back to State Court. The Attorney General appealed the case, and, in April 1975 the appeals court sent it back to Judge Port. The jurist again quickly dismissed the civil action sending it once again back to the State.

In August of 1975, five Realtors of the area and members of COPCA brought suit against Ogden Reid, Commissioner of Conservation and Robert D. Quick, first Deputy Superintendent and Acting Superintendent of the State Police. The jurisdiction was that of Judge Robert Lynch, State Supreme Court, Utica, New York. The plaintiffs were asking for relief in the nature of a mandamus compelling the State to take action to expel the Mohawks from Moss Lake and requiring these officers to criminally prosecute the offenders. Eventually, the judge ruled against the land owners, dismissing the case. He ruled that no authority could be compelled to prosecute against their will.

It seemed that the courts, both State and Federal, did not want to face the issues that would have to be undertaken to properly litigate this matter. Two hundred years of New York State history would have to be examined, including the French and Indian War and the Revolutionary War with England. It would take years, and the writings of historians could not be counted on to be completely accurate. The cloud remained over the Mohawks claim of nine million acres of upstate New York and all of the State of Vermont. Who actually owns the Adirondack Mountains of New York State is yet to be determined.

Another hot potato for the state courts was filed by the Drakes Attorneys in January 1975, asking for damages in the amount of $1,250,000. They accused the state of failure to provide suitable protection for the users of the Big Moose Road in the area of the Ganienkeh Indian encampment. Eventually the State court ruled that the Drakes should have recognized the dangers surrounding Moss lake. The case was dismissed. The Drakes appealed the matter, and once again, the Appeals Court dismissed the action, agreeing with the lower court's decision. If this event occurred today, the courts and/or jury would award in the millions, even though the Drakes may have contributed by their negligence.

The Drake lawsuit was quickly followed by the Madigan's suit against the State. They were only asking for damages in the amount of $750,000, a big mistake. They settled out of court for the sum of $157,000 but, shortly thereafter, realized that it would hardly cover Aprile Madigan's medical expenses. Out of pocket expenses quickly passed the amount awarded and put the family in debt. Mr. Madigan was a bus driver and made only a meager wage, and it appeared that it would take the remainder of his working days to pay back what they owed in medical costs alone. It was doubtful that Aprile could ever return to a normal life and perhaps help to pay some of her medical bills. It was rumored that the doctors in Utica, New York cut their bills in half to help the family through their time of crisis.

Michael Blair, the spokesman for COPCA at the time, served as consultant to the Madigans attorneys during 1975. He stated "In all my years of experience as a newsman, I have never encountered a sadder case than that of Aprile Madigan. The child will suffer both physically and emotionally for the rest of her life. And it is extremely doubtful that those at Ganienkeh, who indiscriminately shot at the car in which she was riding on October 28, will ever be brought to justice. Aprile Madigan is in fact the forgotten victim of irresponsible Indian vengeance against the White man for the injustices of past centuries." (Michael Blair,1977 report to COPCA).

The next hot potato to roll out of the oven was the Mohawks' request of the United Nations to become a member state wholly within the borders of the United States. This is what Ganienkeh wanted so they could have "human rights," which they said was different from "civil rights." The Indians argue that civil rights come from within the system, while human rights can only come from the United Nations through a declaration that Ganienkeh was a country. While asking for their hearing on this matter, they pointed out that the United States helped to restore Okinawa to Japan and other nations in Asia and Africa. They asked why the Native American Indian was the only group denied this right. The AIM organization joined in with Ganienkeh to add muscle to their request.

In early February 1975, the Mohawks at Ganienkeh got the bad news. It first came in the form of several press releases expressing the opinion of the United Nations that the repossession of the Ganienkeh Territory was a "domestic jurisdiction of a member state." This prompted Louis Hall to put his objection to this finding in an official letter to the organization. Hall wrote:

Sehkon:

> The treaties entered into and concluded by the six Nations Confederacy and the United States are an international matter. That only nations that have rights to make treaties is a legal fact. The Dutch, French, English, and later the United States sought treaties with the American Indian. This shows that they were recognized as nations. According to International Law, a nation once recognized as a nation remains a nation until it dissolves itself. No nation may dissolve another nation.

> The United Nations was established to correct and prevent wrongs committed by nations against other nations is a state purpose. This purpose cannot be achieved if only certain nations may benefit from this organization. If peace, harmony and the scourges of war and the end of man's inhumanity to man is to be achieved, then nations should be given the right to benefit from the International United Nations Forum Hearing, hearing the cases of

the oppressed nations. One of the aims of the United Nations is the end of racial discrimination, but in refusing to admit the cases of the oppressed American Indian nations into the United Nations International Forum, wouldn't it be construed by interested observers as racial discrimination being indulged by the United Nations itself? Wouldn't this aid and abet the oppressors?

On December 10, 1948, the United Nations proclaimed its Universal Declaration of Human Rights and it provides in Article 15: "Everyone has the right to a nationality. 2. No one may be arbitrarily deprived of his nationality nor denied the right to change his nationality." No one had the right to deprive us of our Ganienkehecaga Nationality (Mohawk nation, one of the Six Nations Iroquois Confederacy). Ganienkehechaga is the territory of the Mohawk Nation, and has been for countless centuries before the White man came. We were nations long before the fledgling English colonies copied from the Six Nations Confederacy and became the United States nation. We are not an internal matter of any foreign nation, especially one that exists only because of the Red man's land.

We also have the right to man's true estate. We along with other American Indian nations have the right to an independent state on our own land. Some seventy four indigenous nations throughout the world have regained their lands, governments and now decide their own destiny. Only the American Indian is denied this right.

If the United Nations is to bring peace, harmony and rights to all nations, how can they ignore the rights of people on whose defrauded land sits the United Nations itself? Any nation which signed treaties with a member nation of the United Nations should rightfully and automatically qualify to have its case admitted in the United Nations International Court. May wisdom prevail?

Onen
(Signed) Louis Hall
Secretary - GANIENKEH COUNCIL FIRE

Louis Hall added:

BULLETIN!!! THERE IS A MOVEMENT AFOOT TO CREATE ANOTHER UNITED NATIONS WHERE THE OPPRESSED NATIONS WHO WERE REJECTED BY THE UNITED NATIONS CAN TAKE THEIR CASES FOR HEARING.

Hall, further stated regarding the bulletin above: "Wouldn't this be an embarrassment to the United Nations in New York and a doubt cast on its integrity and on its ability to create world peace? About twenty years ago a favorite boast of the American's was that Uncle Sam had the United Nations in his pocket. Only nations approved by the United States may be serviced."

"The United States intention of forcing its jurisdiction on the other party of the treaty constitutes AGGRESSION, INVASION AND USERPATION. It will be resisted by the people of Ganienkeh by every means possible. We shall tell the world how Uncle Sam keeps his word, and what he does to treaties he signs. If treaties are made to be broken, who on earth is safe? If it has to resort to such measures, the United States itself cannot be free! Ganienkeh shall not suffer in silence. The noise shall reverberate around the world and all mankind shall hear." (Ganienkeh Newsletter No #5).

In June 1976 at an Indian meeting at the church of Reconciliation, Utica, New York, a sizzler rolled from the oven. Indian scholar, Gregory Chester, traveled some one hundred miles to attend. He was a teacher of Native American History at Jefferson County Community College in Watertown, New York. He presented a 1922 copy of the Everett Report which had recently been uncovered by Phil Tarbell of the Native American Section of the New York State museum. It seemed that it would have a dramatic effect on the ongoing negotiations and help to remove the cloud over the 1784 Fort Stanwicks Treaty.

Apparently, in 1919, the State legislature authorized a commission to investigate the status of the Mohawk Indian in the State. The commission was headed by Assemblyman Edward Everett and twelve other commissioners. They traveled the State interviewing Mohawks, visiting all reservations of the Iroquois, reviewing written materials and getting verbal recollections of elders. The report outlined what many Whites had feared: That the Mohawks of the Hodenasaunee held title to six million acres of upstate New York. Presumably, this was

New York State land alone and did not involve the State of Vermont. Although some of the others on the commission agreed with its findings, they realized the impact it would have on New York State and slowly disassociated themselves from the commission. When it came time for signing only Everett would sign. The remaining members, five in all, although agreeing with its conclusion, shied away on behalf of the State. After circulation amongst the legislators, the body refused to file it, and without all signatures, it was shelved and the measure soon evaporated. In other words, it was buried by the State. Everett's report read as follows: The adjournment of this meeting together with all the proceedings had heretofore and all research that has been made of the history of the North American Indians, residing in the State of New York, brings us to the conclusion of this investigation and I therefore respectfully submit the result of the findings.

> First: That the Indians residing in the State of New York consummated a treaty with the United States Government, thru its regular channels, the same being approved and ratified by General Washington, at Fort Stanwix, in the State of New York in 1784, by which they were ceded certain territory within the boundaries of said state.

> Second: That the ceding and setting-over to the Indians of this territory was in accordance with and at the conclusion of a treaty consummated by the Indians as a nation and by the United States as a nation.

> Third: I further find that the passing of the title for this ceded territory to the Indians of this state was a legal and proper transaction. And, that the Indians, as a nation, became possessed of the ceded territory, the same as any other nation would become possessed.

> Fourth: I further find that the said Indians of the State of New York, as a nation, are still the owners of the fee simple title to the territory, unless divested of the same by an instrument of equal force and effect as the said treaty of 1784, ceded to them by treaty of 1784.

Although the study was buried, with no reference being made to it anywhere in the Legislature, Mrs. Lulu Stillman, secretary of the Commission, was able to secrete a copy for the future, suspecting that it was a devious attempt by the legislators to cover up the truth. In 1971, during an attempted transfer of land between the State and Akwesasne, the report surfaced. It eventually found its way to Mrs. Helen Upton, Professor Emeritus, Russell Sage College, Troy, New York, and published by her as part of: "The Everett Report In Historical Perspective 1980."

Michael Blair, the public relations man for COPCA, who was at the June 1976 meeting was the only organization to respond to its disclosure, stating: "It was shelved by the Legislature as worthless." It seemed that the State and the Indians both ignored this disclosure, as did the press. What seemed to be one of the most important discoveries of the Moss Lake saga was, purposely ignored. But why? Was Blair right? Or would its disclosure affect the so called sensitive negotiations going on? It would undoubtedly put the State on the defensive. The lack of comment and/or attention given to its disclosure meant that its content was already well known by the negotiators, who did not want to talk about it.

Upton's book delineates the path of the New York Indians from the early 1600's up to and through the 1980's, with particular attention to be given to the Everett Report of 1922. The book seems to treat the Everett investigation as seeking to answer the problem of jurisdiction, whether the Indians were under State or Federal control, and found that the Federal Government was, in fact, the governmental agency responsible for their welfare. Most importantly, the report to the legislature showed, without doubt that the Treaties of 1784 Fort Stanwix, 1789 Fort Harmer and 1794 Fort Stanwix awarded most of the Adirondacks to the Mohawks. (Upton, Helen, the Everett Report in Historical Perspective.)

What appears to be highly unusual is that there is no mention in the book of the 1797 Treaty of Fort Stanwix, wherein the Adirondack land was sold back to the State for $1,000 by Joseph Brandt, the Indian Chief. Was it in the Everett Report papers and Mrs. Upton neglected to mention it, or was it intentionally left out? Was she made to leave it out by a governmental agency? That would be unconstitutional. It certainly would seem that in any dialogue concerning the ownership of the land in question this would be a very important segment. Perhaps, the fact that the Federal Government was the only agency that could deal with Indian affairs, which the Everett Report clearly detailed, meant that Upton did not have to address the 1797 treaty between the Mohawks and the State, as it would be null and void.

Why did the Everett Report have so little bearing on the negotiations? Had a deal been previously made with the Mohawks, and what was happening now was just window dressing? Or, was the sole of the Indian Moccasin now so worn that they were too tired to continue at Moss Lake, and would take what they could get? Or, did the State for the first time come close to admitting that the Brandt Treaty of 1797 was in fact illegal? Whatever the reason, it certainly appears very odd, that at that juncture, more was not made of the Everett Report, and the Brandt Treaty of 1797,(which allegedly sold back the land that was given to the Mohawks by the State.) Perhaps someday the answer will surface, but for now it remains a mystery. Now it is known that the report does exist and what the commission found concerning the Mohawk Indians in New York State.

At this point, it becomes painfully suspicious that the treaty of 1797 (Brandt) was an attempt to defraud the Mohawk Indians of their land by the State of New York, but the courts have found reason to not assume jurisdiction. This issue is truly a "hot potato."

Chapter 19

Sinister Politicians

The saying "Something's fishy in Denmark," reminds one of a smell in Albany, New York, around the spring of 1974, at a time when the Warrior Society had finalized their plans to repossess the Moss Lake Girls' Camp. Maybe it was blowing all the way up from Washington, D.C.?

Michael Blair, COPCA's public relations person, was convalescing from a gall bladder operation and doing a lot of reading, when eureka!, there in the conservative John Birch Society magazine, 1975 addition of "American Opinion," was an article on American Indians called "Red Indians," implying that the American Indian was aligning himself with Communism. The article contained a copy of a letter written by Secretary Louis Hall (Karoniaktajeh), the leader of Ganienkeh, to the head of the militant American Indian Movement (AIM), Dennis Banks. The article was a very informative piece of literature, which answered many outstanding questions that had developed including how the merchants of Old Forge knew in advance that the Mohawks were coming. Some must have been subscribers to the American Opinion magazine. It outlined the recent exploits of an undercover agent for the F.B.I. that had infiltrated the AIM movement and worked his way up to national security officer for the organization of AIM. He must have been quite clever to gain the confidence of the AIM organization and put himself in a position to be privy to all of their intelligence.

He had intercepted a letter sent to Dennis Banks, from Louis Hall dated February 17, 1974. The contents of the letter revealed the Mohawk

Warrior Society's plan to repossess Mohawk land in New York State. This letter was to be kept absolutely secret. It forecast in no uncertain terms the intended movement of the Mohawk Warrior Society in early April 1974, into their ancient homeland of the Adirondack Mountains. The exact site was not mentioned but also included the State of Maine. Hall believed that the land he had in mind was under aboriginal and legal title of the Mohawk Nation. His invitation was to traditional Indians, or those that wished to become traditional, to move onto the land and start a new life. But then he spoke of inViting the Toronto Branch of AIM (American Indian Movement), to train young warriors to defend their homeland and take up roots at the undisclosed location. "We may need manpower," Hall stated, revealing his possible belief that force would have to be used to usurp the land and to defend it from a possible government attack.

After showing the Hall letter to Bank's, he was told to "Burn It." But like any good mole he forwarded the letter to the F.B.1. in Washington. Somehow it found its way to the conservative John Birch Society and there published. Perhaps some bureaucrat saw a way to make a quick buck? Or on the "high road," perhaps someone became privy to a plan to keep it under wraps, didn't like what he was seeing and used the John Birch Society as a way to alert New York State, hopefully unraveling the surprise that was just around the corner?

The F.B.1. it seems, had no choice but to notify official of the BIA (Bureau of Indian Affairs) and then and most importantly the State of New York. That is where things turn very dark and gray. There are nearly three months between February 17th, (the date of the letter) and April 13th, 1974 (the date of the Mohawk's arrival at Moss Lake.) If asked about the letter before its disclosure to the Birch Society, the feds would no doubt deny any knowledge of its existence. No evidence exists that would indicate F.B.I. disclosure of the letter to New York State. Could it have been part and parcel of a State/Federal plan? If it had reached local police it would have been discussed with the Zone Office and Bureau of Criminal Investigation by the Troop Commander. But as it turned out only a last minute notification to the field was made, not leaving sufficient time to formulate a plan of action by the police. It seems that the Warrior Society's movement was not to be interfered with. Suspicions at the time remained very high as they still do today.

During the summer of 1976, the Associated Press interviewed Louis Hall with regard to the letter. Hall confirmed to the media that he had sent the letter. His intent, he explained, was that he wanted to invite as many Indians as possible to participate. In newsletter nine from Ganienkeh, dated February 10th, Hall admits that the content of the letter were his words.

Mike Blair of COPCA, who exposed the embarrassing letter's existence, asked a local F.B.I. agent if the material went to the State Police. The agent replied, "It goes without saying, that the FBI, if in possession of such material, would make it available to the police agency directly involved." (Mike Blair -1976 report to COPCA).

The agent was absolutely right that the F.B.I. should have forwarded such material to the Police Agency involved, but did they? If another agenda presented itself, they may have kept the letter for themselves. This leaves four possible scenarios to consider:

a. The letter and accompanying material was intercepted by the Bureau of Indian Affairs (BIA) and they were working with their counterparts in Canada to solve the problem of the Warrior Society in that country, which was quickly getting out of hand. Perhaps they worked out a plan that would benefit both sides of the border. So the letter went no further.

b. The F.B.I. kept the letter under wraps to see if they could somehow, in the last minute, pull off some saving action that would get great press for the agency or, perhaps some other hidden agenda. Once the John Birch Society published it, the letter would have lost its value to them.

c. The letter was turned over to New York State authorities, perhaps to the attorney general or the Superintendent of State Police, and for some unknown reason, the State wanted, or already knew that the Mohawks were coming, and did not care. Perhaps, the Government took part in bringing the Indians into the State. This may have been done in concert with the Federal government and Canada.

d. When the State learned of the coming invasion, Governor Malcolm Wilson was running for re-election and was afraid that more bloodshed in New York during his term would severely dampen his chances of regaining the Governorship. But there were many ways that the State Police could have prevented bloodshed (i.e. overwhelming force on a roadway during daylight hours).

With regard to scenario (a), concerning the Bureau of Indian Affairs: After the Caughnawaga insurrection in 1972, in Canada, Jean Chretien, representing the Canadian Government said: "I know there are some Americans here trying to stir up trouble, and I think it is not their business and they should not be here. I also know that the Canadian Indians are old enough and big enough to defend their own rights and they don't need out-side help." (Mike Blair 1976 report to COPCA.)

It seemed that Cretien was referring to Louis Hall, the leader of the emerging new era Warrior Society and his followers. Hall was thought of as a U.S. Indian. It would seem that the Canadian government would have been in contact with the BIA of the U.S. to help solve their problem of U.S. Indians causing trouble in Canada.

Perhaps, the State politicians decided to make hay from the coming invasion of the warriors and planned to relocate the interlopers to some area of the state where the economy was severely depressed and persuade them to operate a casino there. The law passed by Congress allowed only Indians to operate casinos at that time and was being used as a tool all over the country to invigorate local economies. The Indians at Akwesasne, on the Canadian border with New York, had previously refused to operate a casino as did the Seneca Indians of Western New York. The Governor needed an Indian Nation that would operate a casino in New York State. It was widely known that the Warrior Society advocated casinos. Perhaps, he felt that he could use the invasion of New York State to his advantage?

This leaves open the door for the possible involvement of the State and/or the U.S. Government, one or both of them, orchestrating the Indian incursion from the beginning. If that be the case, it would explain all the liberal "Indian Giving" the Whites had to endure and pay for, including the final settlement made to the Indians. In support of the above theory, the following excerpt is taken from an Onondaga Nation Report titled, "Threats to Traditional Governments," wherein they state: "In 1990 New York State Governor Mario Cuomo suggested Akwesasne Mohawk elected leaders work with the Warrior Society and casino operators in the form of some legal gaming. The alleged conspiracy between the Warriors and the State of New York continued as certain New York politicians and business leaders wanted to use the Iroquois to introduce casinos to New York State. They felt that if the Iroquois casinos were allowed to flourish, then the New York State Legislature might be more inclined to support state-wide casinos. Cuomo informed the traditional Chiefs that the Iroquois were going to have casinos whether they wanted them or not. The warriors were willing partners in this abuse of our collective sovereignty."

This would indicate that the Mohawk Nation as a whole did not want gambling to infect their Nation and that only the Warrior Society was so inclined. The State needed the Warrior Society to introduce and push gambling on the non-traditional Mohawk people. But then, once here in the United States, and secure in their stronghold of Ganienkeh, the Mohawks once again explored the possibility of repossession of the disputed nine million acres, even publicly announcing it. This probably was their hidden agenda all along, if the State helped to orchestrate their coming. This must have scared the Feds, the State and the courts to no end.

Consider this:
1. Why didn't we stop the Mohawks before they entered Moss Lake? Zone Sergeant Gallo was in place had the plans and resources ready, or,
2. Why didn't we beforehand study that possibility, knowing they were coming, to see if the Warriors could be prevented from entering Moss Lake without bloodshed? After all, it is one hundred percent sure that the State and the federal government knew the insurrection was going to take place.
3. Why were the Warriors not afraid to travel with their women and children and to enter Moss Lake?
4. Why was ranger Bill Marleau told to leave the Indians alone by his superiors when he tried to evict the Mohawks?

5. Why were they allowed to break the many laws of the State (thirty two the first summer as tallied by COPCA), additionally, breaking the conservation laws when they weren't even on the defacto acreage.
6. Why did the Department of Environmental Conservation enlarge the Indians area to nearly five thousand acres of State land?
7. Why were they allowed to cut timber in the forest preserve almost anywhere close to the Moss Lake encampment?
8. Why weren't the Indians responsible for the Drake and Madigan shooting brought to trial?
9. And why did Cuomo's negotiations not force the Mohawks to allow for a State Police Investigation of the shootings?
10. Why were the Indians allowed to dictate to Mario Cuomo what land they wanted and how much?
11. Why were the courts afraid to litigate the land claims of the Indians?
12. Why did the Governor continue to pay the State Police for nearly four years while the political machine sputtered?
13. And why wasn't the Everett report ever taken into consideration. Could the Warrior Society have been privy to something that would severely embarrass the State?
14. To continue the trend of "Indian Giving," Mario Cuomo, in the words of a member of COPCA, "Gave away the farm to satisfy the Mohawks." The farm involved the establishment of the "Turtle Island Trust" for the purpose of obtaining seven hundred acres in one tract and another five thousand acres in another. This land was purchased with private funds. Whose private funds were they?
15. In an effort to obtain the State Police report on this matter, the request was denied. Gallo offered to allow the State Police the opportunity to review this book for sensitive matters and/or investigative technique disclosure prior to publishing. Still, the request was denied.

The Turtle Island Trust Agreement was made on the 25th day of July, 1977. The parties to the trust were Ann Louise Maytag (air to the Maytag fortune), Robert S. Charland and Jon L. Regier. This land was located in the town of Altona, Clinton County, adjacent to the Canadian border. The land possessed a lake and land that the Mohawks could farm and cut timber and actually return to their traditional way. To this day, members of COPCA will swear that the Mohawks were given a considerable amount of money to satisfy their claim to get them out of Moss Lake. They have no proof of this, but they feel strongly that money, in the end, is what finally solidified the deal. If that accusation is correct, then a clear violation of the New York State Constitution had been committed by New York State, unless or course it came from the Federal Government.

It is quite interesting to note that this settlement was so designed as to have no effect on the Warrior Society's main claim to nine million acres of upstate New York and all of the State of Vermont, which remains an unresolved issue. The agreement was not signed by anyone from the State, Federal government or anyone representing Ganienkeh. It's almost as though no agreement or settlement ever occurred and there never was a Ganienkeh at Moss Lake. But it sure seemed like three years of "trick or treat" with the State dolling out the candy.

The following is joint statement by Secretary Cuomo and Kakwirakeron:

On May 13, 1974, a band of Mohawk Indians came down from Canada and took over a 600 acre campsite on state land at Moss Lake, about 50 miles north of Utica and west of Lake Placid. The Indians wanted to reestablish a base for a Mohawk Nation and live a traditional existence on the land, which they believed rightfully belong to them. Tensions at the time were high.

The State took issue with that claim and instituted court proceedings to ascertain who owned the land. Negotiations were also begun to achieve a just and peaceful settlement that could bring dignity to both sides. For more than two years these negotiations were fruitless. In August of 1976, Governor Cary asked Secretary of State Mario Cuomo to be his chief negotiator.

Today, Mr. Cuomo and Kakwirakeron, spokesperson for the Mohawks, are pleased to announce that a settlement to this long dispute has been reached. While the issue of land ownership remains, a new era of relations between Native Americans and other Americans has begun. For the first time in this century a state has been able to work out its problems with its Indian residents peacefully.

Under terms of the agreement, the Indians will leave Moss Lake within the next few months, and move to a site in nearby Clinton County purchased with private funds. The state will provide additional sites in Clinton County—one under lease, the other under revocable permit--on which the Indians will carry out hunting, fishing, reforestation and other activities that are a part of their traditional lifestyle.

In return, the Indians will provide the people of the State of New York with the access to a model traditional community, organized and maintained by the Indians to demonstrate educationally the Indian way of life. Mr. Cuomo and Kakwirakeron believe this settlement will heighten sensitivities on both sides and will give a greater appreciation to all Americans for what the Indian has contributed to the nation and how little he has received in return.

The agreement stipulates that the Indians will begin leaving Moss Lake no later than August 1, 1977, and complete the move within ninety days. Between now and August, both the Indians and the State will meet with religious leaders and political leaders and others to help develop an atmosphere of cooperation.

Both Secretary Cuomo and Kakwirakeron are confident that the people of Clinton County will find the Mohawks not only good neighbors but a boon to the area rather than a burden.

And both spokesmen wish to thank the American Arbitration Association for keeping the negotiations moving in the right direction.

Finally, both spokesmen wish to note the good offices of Governor Cary. His one mandate was that the agreement should be reached "without the use of force." The achievement of that goal should be a source of overriding satisfaction to everyone.

It should be noted that no apology was ever made to the members of COPCA or the people of Big Moose or to the victims of the attempted murders, by either, Cuomo, Governor Carey, the Feds or the Indians that injured the Whites.

Chapter 20

Gun-Shy

The little blonde girl hurriedly, half ran, half walked, into the Herkimer State Police Station ahead of her parents. An observer would quickly realize that something of a physical nature was impairing her ability to run full gate. If she was able to she would. Also apparent, was the fact that something of an urgent nature was motivating her hurriedness. The Troopers had called and said, "we have something for you Aprile." She ran into the squad room and stopped quickly with her hand over her mouth as she observed a new Schwinn bicycle and a Patten leather saddle for the horse in her future. By this time she had become very fond of the Troopers and wanted all the more to be one when she grew up.

Gun-Shy is a term used by Aprile Madigan to define how she and her family felt after the horrendous attack by the Mohawk Warrior Society on October 28, 1974. Reference is made to chapters 1 "The Runnin Gears of Hell" and Chapter 9 "Circle the Wagons" wherein the awful events of this unprovoked attack are outlined. The dictionary defines Gun-Shy as "afraid of loud noises (gunfire), being markedly distrustful, afraid or cautious." To this day these effects linger with Aprile and her family and would remain with anyone who was the victim of attempted murder in such a vicious way. Not since the era of Bonnie and Clyde (the notorious bank robbers of the early 20th century) has so much gunfire been directed towards one car. Perhaps the days of Elliot Ness in Chicago when the gang wars were at their peak would also parallel the shooting events at Moss lake.

The Madigan family operated a small farm outside of Phelps, New York, a small town adjacent to Geneva. Aprile was a tall slender girl of nine with green eyes and blonde hair. She had to wear glasses to correct her vision, which she hated very much, but she was much too humble to admit that she was very cute. Pictures of her at that age tell the real story. She had grown up with her brother Steven who was three years older and taught her to play with trucks and other boy things. Aprile was somewhat of a Tomboy because of this, but early on fell in love with horses, visiting her neighbors equines almost daily. She loved animals very much and had two pets, "Snoopy her dog and Chocolate the cat."

Aprile was nine years old when this tragedy occurred. The family had been on vacation in Vermont and returned to Big Moose, New York to visit friends. They had dinner at the Glenmore Hotel in Big Moose and were heading out of the wilderness towards Eagle Bay when the Indian attack took place. The family had no knowledge of the Indian problem lurking at the Moss Lake Girls' Camp. The Madigan car limped in to the State Police roadblock at Eagle Bay with two flat tires, leaking gasoline from a punctured gas tank and a severally injured little girl.

At St.Lukes Hospital while Aprile lay in her hospital bed recovering, she realized that something had drawn her heart to the New York State Police. She wanted to be a mounted Trooper. Perhaps she had seen a mounted Trooper at the New York State Fair or maybe she had heard of the famous "Grey Riders" (mounted Troopers) who in 1917 set out on horseback to enforce the laws of the State. A young Trooper had been assigned to look after Aprile while she was at the hospital. He had watched her lay there and suffer for days before she regained consciousness enough to carry on a conversation. The girl told the young officer how she wanted to be a mounted Trooper when she grew up. This apparently touched his heart and he ripped the State Police patch from his shoulder, giving it to Aprile. She has the patch to this day and always tells the story of the young Trooper, when she looks at her treasure in her scrap book. Her second choice in life was to become a nurse, which she became after recovering from her injuries. It seemed that she was drawn to an occupation wherein she could help her fellow man.

Indian Givers

When the press entered the picture, their harassment became unbearable for the Madigan family. One reporter was particularly pushy in an effort to get verbal statements from the family. After several warnings he continued to harass them and eventually had to be evicted from the hospital by the trooper assigned there. But the media was not finished by any means. One night a reporter somehow obtained a lab coat and put it over his clothing and his camera. With stealth, he made it by the nurses' station and slipped into Aprile's room, taking pictures of the little girl suffering in her bed. After learning of this disgusting move, the nurses quickly relocated her to a room directly across from their station so they could monitor everyone who entered. This was only the start of Aprile's extreme dislike for all news media, which she disliked even more than she did the Indians.

After a short time, Aprile learned that she had been shot by the Mohawk Warriors Society and began to suffer nightmares of Indians at her windows and in the halls, waking up screaming. When awake, shadows often spooked her. Drapes and curtains had to be kept drawn and medications administered, to help her through the turmoil she was suffering.

After approximately one month, she was allowed to go home for Thanksgiving. Her mother worried about the bullet next to her heart, believing that if she moved too vigorously, the projectile could shift and cause her death. But Jean was dealing with a nine year old who couldn't stay down and had been confined to a bed in the hospital for a long period of time. She was acting somewhat like a kitten or puppy when they first find their legs. Mother got through it, suffering motherly anxiety while Aprile was home.

When the little girl regained enough strength, she returned to the hospital three months later to have the remaining bullet removed. After another successful operation by Dr. Idelhoch and a long period of convalescence, she was again allowed to go home, (taking a full year to return to something of a normal life.) She has nothing but praise for the doctors and nurses of St. Lukes Memorial with regard to her care. She speaks of one nurse in particular, a tall blonde who saw to her every need. To this day, she wonders who she was and how she could somehow repay her for care and understanding. Hopefully that day will come.

The members of COPCA and the children of Big Moose, along with WKTV in Utica, sponsored a most successful benefit for Aprile and her family. This was followed closely by the Greyhound Bus Drivers collecting money and stuffed animals. The State Troopers of Zone One bought her a beautiful new bicycle for her use after her recovery and a saddle for that horse of the future. Some of her doctors had also cut their bills to help the family.

Then, from around the corner, came another shocker. The insurance company would not pay for the repairs to the Madigan car. The agent stated that criminal mischief was an exclusion in the policy and, therefore, they could not pay the claim. The car had to be junked but the Madigans were responsible for the remaining balance owed to the finance company.

The family was forced to sue the State in an effort to recover some of their debt and suffering. They asked the State for $750,000 and were awarded a mere $157,000 by the court to settle the case. After paying for associated costs and lawyer fees they were left with a huge negative bottom line. The family was deep in debt and it was doubtful at this time that Aprile could ever assist with the financial situation.

The Madigans had all suffered a great deal as result of this tragedy in their lives but agree that time has helped to heal the wounds. Scars remain, particularly with Aprile. Unless one has been exposed to front line combat or something of even greater impact, there can be no understanding of "The Runnin Gears of Hell" that this family and the Drakes went through. Envision being under extreme gunfire at close range from four sides and trapped in an automobile. No thanks!

Roger, Jean and Steven all endured the Indian onslaught, suffering along with Aprile. They sat at her side in the hospital and prayed for her recovery. When she was released and at home they continually feared that the bullet would move and cause her death. They too were left with the symptoms of being gun-shy. They retained some fear of Indians, believing that there were good Indians and bad Indians.

Steven was Aprile's twelve year old brother who also suffered the unprovoked attack and the aftermath of the event. He was sent home to live with neighbors while his sister was in the hospital and worried day and night about her survival. That's when he learned to pray and had to endure the many questions thrown at him about the shooting, like, "How does it feel to be shot at?" and "Are you afraid of Indians?" He has suffered very little from the harrowing event and realizes that there are good and bad in all races of the world, so he holds no grudges against the Redman.

After Aprile recovered enough to ride, she and the family, although very anxious, drove by the Mohawk stronghold. Indian horses were in an old corral next to the Big Moose Road. Aprile became very upset and angered when she realized that the horses were very gaunt and no doubt underfed. That scene bothered her more than actually being shot by the braves.

The Mohawk Warrior Society never offered any sympathy for what they had done. No flowers, no cards, no visits to the hospital. Perhaps they were so instructed by their legal counsel, fearing that they would show a degree of guilt if this was done. However, the Chiefs of the Iroquois Nation did state to the press that they were praying to the Great Spirit for the recovery of the Drake and Madigan families.

The prayers of the people in Aprile's life and perhaps those of the Iroquois certainly helped for her to have a near normal life. Her recovery led to marriage and three children, two boys and a girl, of whom she is very proud.

It took a great deal of courage for Aprile to come forward and cooperate with the authors of this book. She has had to re-live the events and aftermath of that night in Eagle Bay, carrying the scars that go along with being a victim of an attempted murder. Her wishes are to remain unknown as the victim of this assault and to be left alone for the remainder of her days on this earth.

CHAPTER 21

THE CONCLUSION

    The chilling but beautiful call of the loon could once again be heard on Moss Lake in the early fall of 1978. A lone doe stood on the shoreline. Her look seemed to be one of suspicion as she viewed the opposite side of the lake. The aborigines were now gone and the land had almost returned to the Adirondack wilds that it once was. All that remained of man's presence was the foundations and scrap lumber of the Girls Camp buildings the Mohawks took with them and the charred remains of the club house which had burned in the winter of 1977. They left behind many memories, some good and some bad, of the nearly four year occupation of the Moss Lake Girls' Camp. In the years to come, those memories would be the material for many stories and tales of the Indians' presence there, and with time, they would grow larger and better with each telling.

    The agreement made between New York State and the Mohawk Warrior Society in early May 1977 was accomplished without the use of force to evict the Indians and no further injuries occurred. The agreement became an additional act of Indian Giving by the State and a possible violation of the State's Constitution. The manner in which it was drawn up, giving the Indians the use of two parcels of land in the Altona area and the establishment of a trust would not be a constitutional problem because the land was not actually given to the Mohawks. The removal of the Moss Lake Buildings by the Indians would seem to be contrary to the mandates of that piece of legislation. State Senator James H. Donovan stated that the handling of the Moss

Lake seizure was "one of the most disgraceful pages in New York State history." Donovan, who vehemently opposed the Indian takeover from the beginning and sided with COPCA's efforts to dislodge the Mohawks also stated that Cuomo's "outrageous giveaways of taxpayers' property are a flagrant violation of the Constitution that Cuomo now wants to swear to uphold as Lieutenant Governor." (Crystal Courier8/3/78)

The Mohawks agreed to leave the Moss Lake site by no later than November 1977. However the completion of the dismantling and removal of the buildings did not occur until late summer of 1978. These building materials were transported to their new Ganienkeh in the Town of Altona, Clinton County. It is presumed that their cache of weapons, including those that injured the two whites went along and are now somewhere in Clinton County or Canada.

The members of COPCA and other local land owners were elated when the last Mohawk left Moss Lake. They were the people who suffered the most because of the State's inept handling of the entire matter, except of course Aprile Madigan and her family and Stephen Drake and his family.

COPCA, along with most other Whites of Big Moose and the Altona area, believe that one of the reasons the Indians were able to get what they wanted was because they were able to dupe the press. The press, through favorable coverage, put additional pressure on the State to settle favorably with the Mohawks. COPCA lists the following amongst additional reasons why the Moss Lake occupation was sustained:

1. The image of down trodden people that has been presented to New Yorkers by the media.
2. The existence of a woefully small, but vocal support group that somehow manages to get media coverage.
3. The refusal of the media to present all the facts of the matter about the renegades on editorial pages according to the image perpetuated in news accounts.
4. The passing of the buck by both State and Federal Courts.
5. The numbers of the opposition. The only really concerned was a handful of people at Big Moose and other property owners surrounding the state site. If no one is demanding that the state

throw the renegades out except this small number, a Brooklyn Governor who does not know an Indian from a shoehorn loses little politically by letting them stay. However he loses quite a bit if the first renegade gets his hair mussed by State Police. (Landsman - page 48).

The members of COPCA, in a memo to reveal the hypocrisy of Ganienkeh, stated: "The notion that the Indians are returning to, and preserving nature is a sham. Photos taken by the Rome Sentinel reveal piles of trash at Moss Lake, some taken while the Mohawks were there and others taken after the Indians had left. Other photo's reveal several junked cars." "Returning to nature presumably means using nature's water to wash your cloths. Although the Moss Lake site contains Moss Lake, which is full of water, the Indian women choose to use the Laundromat in Eagle Bay. The renegades have three separate telephone listings." One member of COPCA, who asked to remain anonymous, readily admitted that the Mohawks benefitted from the opposition they received from the locals. He stated, "I guess we really were an ally of the Indians but didn't realize it until towards the end."

This four year occupation of the Moss Lake Girls' camp by the Mohawk Warrior Society brought out the best of certain individuals. Trooper Bill Chesebro rose to the challenge he was given by Major Charland. Reporter John Isley of the Boonville Herald covered the many commendations that Bill received concerning his performance during this time. Included within the article were excerpts from the commendation of Dr. Joseph Stuhlberg, of the American Arbitration Association, and also from Major Robert Charland and Major William F. Keefe, who replaced Charland upon his retirement as Troop Commander of Troop "D". Additionally, Chesebro was made an honorary member of the Warrior Society. Perhaps, some of the credit that has been dealt out, should go to Bill's wife Ruby, who put up with the late night calls, and the many hours of Bill's absence because of Indian affairs, and who entertained the Mohawk's that Bill brought home for meals etc.. In most Police Departments in the United States, the actions of Chesebro would have brought an automatic promotion. That sort of performance is what the Troopers expected from their members in that era.

Another important asset of the State Troopers was Chief Robert (Bob) Crofoot of the Town of Webb Police Department. He and members of his department were present at most times of crisis and assisted the Troopers, as needed. The State Police felt secure knowing that Bob and his men were there for the asking, and his advice was always taken into account. He had been in the Police business for a long time and nothing can replace years of experience of a busy Policeman.

Barney Barnum, the Superintendent of Camp Gorham and a part time Environmental Officer, stood out amongst the local people for his involvement in the Moss Lake fiasco. It seemed that when a crisis would erupt, there was Barny to lend assistance. Very noteworthy was his every day care of the Troopers needs (wood, water, coffee and occasionally donuts) at the fixed posts. Barney and his wife Betty were very active members of the COPCA organization, and living next door to Ganienkeh, they had to endure many negative events that occurred such as the Indian's cattle on their property almost daily. Barney was an excellent representative of the Department of Conservation and the COPCA organization.

Doug Bennett, president of COPCA, his wife Bonnie and his family must also receive accolades for their never ending efforts to bring the Mohawk incursion to a successful end. The pressure they and the rest of COPCA put on the State was constant, and resulted in jump starting the negotiations when they would stall. Also, we have to consider the three years of anxiety and disruption that their lives took on while the politicians, for the most part, ignored their pleas for help and understanding, while the people of Big Moose raised their families.

Art Montour (Kakwirakeron) the spokesperson and one of the leaders of the Mohawk Warriors Society, early on established a rapport with State Troopers and quickly secured the necessary staples for the Mohawks' initial existence. He became the leading force of the Indians' insurrection displaying much zeal to reach his goals. It is believed that Montour, Louis Hall and other leaders of the Warrior Society wished to accomplish their goals without bloodshed. His lectures throughout the state brought many organizations to the side of the Indians and a better understanding of two hundred years of Indian oppression. Most of all, his negotiations with New York State secured the land for the new Ganienkeh and has set an everlasting precedent for the future of the American Indian when negotiating with government officials. It is believed that Montour, Hall and their followers, opened the floodgates for a prosperous future for the American Indian.

We have to tip our hats to the above listed individuals and their spouses. Their efforts must be recognized and applauded by all sides of this dispute.

Stephen and Michael Drake have recovered from their wounds and have led fairly normal lives, although Stephen is still bothered by his injuries. They both reside with their wives and families in the Adirondack area. Both Drake's own their own successful businesses in the mountains. They are still angry about the State's handling of the Moss Lake affair and are not alone with that feeling.

The biggest losers of the entire event were without a doubt Aprile Madigan and her family. In addition to Aprile's injuries, the huge accumulation of medical bills that faced them in years following the Moss Lake incursion was overwhelming. To this day, Aprile has trouble discussing the events that surrounded her injuries and her recovery. The biggest positive thing that has occurred in her life is that she survived this horrible event with only a few emotional problems, and was able to marry, and mother three children. She appears to be very happy with her present life and speaks of the future with bright hopes. She remains adamant that her identity and location remain a secret with the writers of this book.

The biggest winners, in fact the only winners of the Moss Lake insurrection were the "Mohawk Warrior Society" and the American Indian in general. The Warriors gained the land for their Ganienkeh and set a very powerful precedent for the future of all entitled Indians in the United States. The State's attempt at a lawsuit, (N.Y. State vs. Danny White Et al), to remove the cloud over the land ownership of the nine million acres, lies dormant somewhere in the files of an upstate New York Court. It seems to be the forbidden litigation of the 20th century.

As result of the Moss Lake incursion, the Warriors learned that they could, in fact, push the mighty Empire State around. This emboldened them with power which they took with them to their new Ganienkeh on the Canadian border. On the negative side for the Indians, the activities of the Warrior Society after Moss lake, has resulted in their power causing turmoil throughout the Mohawk Nation. It invigorated the never ending disputes between the Indian factions, mostly perpetuated by the Warriors, between the Iroquois, the United States, local governments and Canadian governments. It further emboldened AIM since the inception of the Moss lake incursion, and it has been reported that AIM instigated twelve separate bombings and other small takeovers throughout the United States and Canada during the time of the Mohawks repossession of the girls' camp. The Warrior Society failed to keep a low profile after their achievement at Moss Lake and did not rest on their laurels. Instead, they became more active in their new home and their influence could once again be felt throughout Iroquois Territory.

This story did not end at Moss Lake. On the affirmative side it was just the beginning of reparations to the aborigine. The Indian was awarded land claims and/or monetary settlements, including the establishment of many Indian casinos all over the country from that time forward.

Life goes on in the Central Adirondacks and particularly in the area of Moss Lake, Big Moose Lake, Bubb Lake and Sis Lake. Tourists invade the area during all seasons, many not even aware of the Grace Brown Murder and the insurrection that took place at Moss Lake. The State DEC has transformed the Indian encampment into a remarkable hiking experience. The trails traverse the outskirts of Moss Lake and connect with the Bubb and Sis Lakes. Reportedly, with the help of the military, the DEC has thoroughly swept the area for weapons, booby traps, dynamite, and anything of danger to the general public. Because of the history of the area, many are confident that another bizarre happening is just around the corner, and in the meantime the restless spirit of Grace Brown who was murdered in the area early in the twentieth century and perhaps other restless spirits linger in the area.

Pictured: Senator James Donovan examining the remains of a Moss Lake building removed by the Mohawks

*Pictured on the left is Doug Bennett of Copca,
Senator James Donovan, Newsman, and
Assemblyman Peter Dokuchitz*

'End of a nightmare' for Aprile

BY STELLA CECERE

Christmas in February

Pictured: Inv. Mario Restante (left), Aprile Madigan and Senior Inv. Richard Gildersleeve.

References

INVENTORY OF ARTHUR EINHORN MOHAWK RESEARCH COLLECTION, 1974-1980

Primarily newspaper clippings that document the initial occupation of the Moss Lake territory by the Mohawk Indians and the subsequent developments. Also contains duplicates of the correspondence of parties other than Arthur Einhorn. Also includes various sorts of literature from the Ganienkeh settlement itself, as well as of the numerous organizations that were involved in the controversy, such as AIM, and the Syracuse Peace Council. The bulk of the material consists of newsletters and press releases form the most vocal group in opposition to the occupation, the Concerned Persons of the Central Adirondacks(COPCA),1974-1976.Also contains such miscellaneous items as notes by a student of Einhorn's at a gathering in which the Ganienkeh Indians presented their mission to a group at Jefferson Community College.

Organized with general materials preceding records of opposing and supporting groups.

Contents
Correspondence, re: Moss Lake Occupation, August 1974-October 1975
Ganienkeh Settlement, various letters and press statements, Manifesto, n.d.
"Indian Rights- the Reality of Symbolism" in New York State Bar Journal, Oct. 1978
Mohawk Indians speech, photocopied notes, Nov. 8, 1974
News Clippings, 1974-1978
Newspapers- Akwesasne Notes, Early Winter1973-Early Winter 1974

Opposing Groups- Adirondack Park Agency, clippings, July-Oct. 1975
Opposing Groups- American Opinion article, photocopy, Sept. 1975
Opposing Groups- Church Opposition, clipping, n.d.
Opposing Groups-COPCA-clippings, 1975
Opposing Groups-COPCA-correspondence, 1975
Opposing Groups-COPCA-Court Brief, photocopy, re legal action brought against Commissioner of Environmental Conservation, 1975
Opposing Groups-COPCA-literature, statement of facts, n.d.
Opposing Groups-COPCA-Newsletters, 1975-1976
Opposing Groups-COPCA-Press Releases, . n.d.
Supporting Groups-AIM, general clippings, 1974-1975
Supporting Groups-AIM, photocopy of Hamburg meeting minutes, July 1975
Supporting Groups-ARPA, newsletter, Nov. 1974
Supporting Groups-Council of Churches, clippings, 1975-1976 Groups-Friends of Indians, CT division, clippings and newsletters, 1975
Supporting Groups-North County Children's Clinic, n.d.
Supporting Groups-RAIN-newsletter and clippings, May, 1976, n.d.
Supporting Groups-Syracuse Peace Council, Newsletter and flier, 1975
News Clippings, Feb. 1975-Nov.16, 1976

GANIENKEH NEWS LETTER by Louis Hall (Karoniaktejeh)

Introduction - Who made you?
Mohawk Ten Commandment
What is the warrior society - September 1974
The Greatest Man Who Ever Walked the Earth
To all North American Indians - December 1974
Sure Fire Way to Oppress All Indians - January 1975
Facing Reality - February 1975
Letter to the United Nations - February 1975
The Blair Report - May 1975
Will Wonders Never Cease - May 1975

Message From Ganienkeh (Untitled) - October 1975
To Believe or To Know - October 1975
The Acquiescent Indian - January 1976

MISCELLANEOUS PUBLICATIONS

New York Press - The Warriors Within - Brad Lockwood 2/01/06
    Grand Council of the Iroquois - Complaint to Pres. Ford Nov 74
Robin Caudell - Ganienkeh celebrates 25 years - May 1999
Time Archieve - Trouble in the Land of Flint - Don Sider 1974

Sovereignty and Symbol - Gail Landsman 1988
The Everett Report In Historical Perspective - Helen M. Upton

UNPUBLISHED

The Blair Report
Blair Report to Members of COPCA

Ganienkeh Manifesto

Ganienkeh - Land of the Flint - ancient homeland of the Mohawk Nation, whose descendants, with traditional natives from other Indian nations, are moving back to repossess their natural heritage. Other native nations throughout the world have regained their lands and governments. The North American traditionals are sure that the Government of the United States and its general public shall see the justice and the rights of the American Indian people to such a move.

Ganienkeh shall be the home of the traditional Red man. Here, according to the rights accorded everyone else in the world, the Red man shall exercise his proven government and society according to his culture, customs and traditions. According to the rights of the human, he has the right to operate his state with no interference from any foreign nation or government. Here the people shall live according *to the rules of nature. Here the Great Law of the Six Nations Iroquois Confederacy shall prevail. The people shall live off the land. The co-op system of economy shall prevail. Instead of the people competing with each other, they shall help and co-operate with each other. Here, they shall relearn the superior morality of the ancients.*

It is not a backward step. The way to a proper, moral government, a practical and worthy economic system and a proper, moral human relationship is true progress. What is regarded as progress in this day and age is a road to destruction. Advanced technology abuses nature. The result has been the pollution of air, land, water and the human mind. A brief reflection reveals how abused nature repays in kind. The competitive society. The main objective of human intelligence should be the peace and happiness of mankind on earth, not the profits saturation of a few tycoons and the worship of advanced technology. The kind of progress has brought the world to the brink of destruction.

Let there be a ray of light somewhere. Instead of abuse of nature let there be an appreciation of nature. Ganienkeh calls all native American Indians who wish to live according to their culture, customs, and tradition.

Traditional Indians who answer the call and participate in the project shall be asked to prepare to meet unusual situations. Indians lived a million years without money and technology. They lived off the land. (Today's existing co-operative communities refuse Family Allowance, Welfare relief, Old Age Pension and still live very comfortable. Utilizing the co-op community system, the Indian State of Ganienkeh shall be a money-less state. The requirement is enough land to grow food for all, enough grazing land for beef cattle or buffalo and enough timber land for building materials; and people who are ready to work towards its success.

The Mohawk Land was lost in an earlier century by fraud and its possession by New York State and the State of Vermont constitute illegal usurpation. No deed signed by Joseph Brant and the New York State agent can extinguish the rights of the Mohawks to their own country. The native North Americans not only have the rights but are duty bound to CORRECT THE WRONG COMMITTED BY JOSEPH BRANT AND THE NEW YORK STATE AGENTS AGAINST THE MOHAWK NATION. No individual Indian nor any individual Nation of the Six Nations Confederacy has the right to sell or give away land without the consent of the Grand Council of the Six Nations confederacy. This was one of the findings of the N.Y. Senate investigating commission which ended in 1922.

Joseph Brant, who was not even a member of the Six Nations Confederacy having before disqualified himself, did on March 29, 1797, with an alleged "power of attorney" make a deal with the New York State in which he gave away all the Mohawk land to the said New York State. Several months before in November of 1796, the same Joseph Brant with the same "power of attorney" gave away large tracts of land in Ontario to his British friends. It was called 999-year leases at no cost, that is, no revenue was to accrue. Brant loved white people so much or was mesmerized by them that he pauperized outright, his own people to please his white friends.

In a letter to the representatives of the United Nations at San Francisco, California, April 13, 1945, the Six Nations Confederacy states strongly that Joseph Brant was never given the right to give away their lands. Even if they had given Brant the alleged _power of attorney_ it still would be invalid as the deal would have to be consummated in the Grand Council of the Six Nations Confederacy. The fee simple is still vested in the Six Nations and the Mohawks have the aboriginal title to ancient Kanienkeh. No self respecting nation on earth would accept the dirty deal handed out by Joseph Brant and the New York State agents.

The Mohawk Nation, supported by traditional North American aboriginal natives from other native nations such as Ojibways, Crees, Algonquin's and others, shall move into the Mohawk homeland of Ganienkeh. The combined nations shall establish the Independent North American Indian State of Ganienkeh. The Great Law - Gayanerekowa - which has lately spread all over native North America shall be the Constitution of the Independent North American Indian State of Ganienkeh. The Mohawk Nation is not breaking away from the Iroquois Confederacy. It is repossessing its homeland with the help of other Red Indian traditionals and at the same time exercising its human rights accorded everyone else in the world. Other native nations of Asia and Africa have regained lost lands and human rights. The United States restored Okinawa to Japan. We expect that the United States should see their way to render the same justice to American Indians.

To any premise that the Mohawk project is an internal matter of a white people's government certain steps are hereby taken along with pointing out that the Indian Nations have long had their own organized governments and society, greatly preceding the people who have taken by usurpation authority of this area of the world and these steps include declaring to the world, news of this move on the part of the traditional Indians of North America. There shall be communication to every nation on earth and to their embassies at the United Nations with a request of foreign relations with the countries contacted, even if only on paper. That the Indian State of Ganienkeh has this right is guaranteed by the United Nations as the same right has been provided to new nations, who are actually old ones who have formerly been likewise defrauded of their land and governments.

The U.S. is a member of the United Nations and sworn to uphold its principles. The U.N. proclaimed its Universal Declaration of Human Rights in December 1948 and it provides in Art. 15: (1) Everyone has the right to a nationality. (2) No one may be arbitrarily deprived of his nationality nor denied the right to change his nationality.

We too are human and should have the rights accorded everyone else in the world; the right to our nationality, the right of our nation to exist and *the right to an area of land for our own territory end state where we can exercise our own proven government and society.*

Notices shall also be sent to the President of the United States and to the Governors of the States of New York and Vermont. A request for foreign relations will be submitted to the U.S. Government. The procedure being followed to regain the ancient Mohawk homeland is consistent with human rights. Nature did not give certificates of possession to people she consigned to certain areas. Ours is the strongest naturally legal right known to man, aboriginal right.

Message to Congress, July 8, 1970.

"The first Americans the Indians are the most deprived group in our nation. On virtually every scale of measurement, employment, income, education health - the condition of the Indian people ranks at the bottom. This condition is the heritage of centuries of injustices ... The American Indians have been oppressed and brutalized, deprived of their ancestral lands and denied the opportunity to control their own destiny."

—President Richard M. Nixon

Today's white man say that the injustice was done two centuries ago and it has nothing to do with him. The present Mohawk action is in 1974 and will the white man continue to keep justice from the Indians? The Mohawk project is the way to real self determination - control their own destiny. It is the way for the Red Indian race to regain lost pride, lost belief in humanity and to offset escapes from reality like alcohol, drugs, and suicides that are destroying the Indian people.

From the PREAMBLE TO THE CONSTITUTION OF THE UNITED NATIONS
1 4 5 0
(circa?)
O N O N D A G A

I am Deganawidah and with the Five Nations Confederate Rotiyaner I place the Tree of the Great Peace....Roots have spread out from the Tree of

Great Peace...and the name of these roots is the Great White Roots of Peace. If any man or any nation outside of the Five Nations shall show a desire to obey the laws of the Great Peace....they may trace the root to their source... and they shall be welcomed to take shelter beneath the Tree....

1 9 4 5 SAN FRANCISCO

We the peoples of the United Nations determined to save succeeding generations from the scourges of war...and to reaffirm faith in fundamental human rights...and to establish conditions under which justice and respect for law can be maintained ... do hereby establish an international organization to be known as the United Nations.

The noblest work of man is to find the formula for peace and happiness for everyone on earth. To that end the most urgent needs of the nation of mankind are proper, moral governments, a practical economic system that eliminates poverty and advanced human relationship. Down through the ages, the world's wisest men have ever tried to find a formula of peace and happiness for suffering and deprived humanity. We've read of the efforts of Socrates, Plato, Aristotle and many others. Wise as they were, they all failed in this, mankind's greatest work.

Searchers for the formula have consulted the Holy Scriptures for instructions on devising a proper, moral government, but the teachers in the Good Book only spoke of Kingdoms, which are total dictatorships and had no idea of the government of, for and by the people. As no one has the right to be king or queen, it showed no idea of truly proper human relationships. Not knowing how to eliminate poverty, the holy teachers advocated poverty. Ask starving Indians in Northern Ontario reserves of destitute areas in Indian if they are happy and at peace. They repress people in the last stages of poverty and live in absolute misery and wretchedness. The Holy Scriptures laid no claim to have a formula for peace and happiness on earth, only in the "after-life" - after you're dead. That's no good for people suffering the tortures of the damned in this life.

The East had its own famous wise men, among whom was Confucius. As they were, they too could not find the key to peace and happiness, a proper moral government, a practical economic system and human relationship. It took the North American Deganawidah to find the formula. He took from natural righteousness (Kariwiyo) and made a Code which he called

Gayanerekowa - known as the Law of the Great Peace. The Wise Man of the ages, armed only with his Great Law, conquered the five most fierce nations imaginable in history; the Mohawks, Oneidas, Cayugas, Senecas and the Onondagas, united them in a Confederacy (Kanonsonnionwe in Mohawk), put them symbolically in one Long House and created peace and happiness that lasted until the white man came with his Dark Age. Gayanerekowa was the world's first national Constitution and the first international law, the first code of human rights. The Iroquois Confederacy was the worlds first people's republic with sovereignty for everyone. All other countries were kingdoms and in a kingdom only the monarch has sovereignty. Everything and everyone belonged to the king. The entire world may thank the Peacemaker Deganawidah for whatever rights and freedoms its people enjoy, BUT not all the rights and freedoms in the Great Law were adopted. The copiers kept full justice from their people. They left loopholes through which they may continue subtly to oppress humanity....

There has been a continuous psychological warfare waged against the American Indian. It's every bit as deadly as the one with guns. The casualties are the drunks, drug addicts, suicides, renegades and traitors, all destroyed people. Indians are made to feel cheap and inferior. It results in identity conflict. Most Indians cannot find' work in what man's mainstream and have to go on welfare relief and are called _welfare bums_ to help them slide down in their self valuation.

The establishment of the Independent North American Indian State of Ganienkeh offers a positive solution of the problems of Indians. They get away from the deleterious effects of welfare relief life. They can get away from the slums of cities. They will live in fresh unpolluted air. They shall help build an Indian State. They shall regain privileges. They shall do it themselves. No longer shall white man's government say Indians are a burden on their country's economy via welfare relief. A well run cooperative community needs no financial help whatever. The white man will no longer be hurt where it hurts the most, in the pocket book. Wouldn't that alone be an inducive persuasion to the white man to let go the captive Indians? There may be some broken down brainwashed Indians who because of fear and inferiority complex shall be afraid to go to Ganienkeh- at first.

The vanguard of strong, resolute men, women and children who shall establish the Indian State are traditionals. They know their rights are exercising it. The establishment of the Indian State gives the North

American Indians an international personality and the right to establish foreign relations with other nations - all the rights mentioned above are guaranteed by the United Nations. Because of the nature of the movement, it is an international affair, not an internal matter.

The prospective members of the new Indian State shall be ready to use herbal preventative medicine, to keep sickness to a minimum (see Chief Smallboy's healthy camp). By following the above, the Independent North American State of Ganienkeh shall be free of the white man. For the protection of the rights, culture, customs and traditions of the Indian people who participate and join in the project, the following is proposed:

ARTICLES OF AGREEMENT
BY THE NATIONS WITHIN THE
INDEPENDENT NORTH AMERICAN INDIAN STATE OF GANIENKEH
PLEDGE OF ALLIANCE

Assembled this day on repossessed Mohawk land, representatives of various North American Indian Nations have come to agreements with the host Mohawk Nation in matters attending the establishment of the Independent North American Indian Nations agreed on the following:

1. That the host Mohawk Nation was dispossessed of its land by unjust actions on the part of a foreign people and its repossession was a result of a joint effort of the above mentioned Indian Nations whose signatures appear below; therefore the said North American Indian Nations concerned shall share in equality the benefits, protection, privileges resources, production and the government of the said Independent North American Indian State of Ganienkeh
2. That the assembled North American Indian Nations do make ordain and publish an A L L I A N C E and take the Pledge on the Wampum that they shall forever defend and protect each nation in the Alliance and the Great Law of the Six Nations Iroquois Confederacy, mankind's first and greatest national constitution.
3. That the assembled Indian Nations shall implement the Co-operative economic system to run the Independent North American Indian State of Ganienkeh and that each member nation shall

take a certain area to lock its co-operative communities and that every subject of the said Independent North American Indian State of Ganienkeh is a member of the co-op, with the right to an equal share of the production and to this end, every subject of the said Independent North American Indian State of Ganienkeh shall pledge to do his share of the work to so earn his share of the production.

4. *That the assembled Indian Nations shall live off the land, grow food on every available acre, keep livestock and preserve the environment.*
5. *That each member Nation continue to exercise its own customs and traditional Indian spiritual ceremonies and each member Nation shall permit the other members to adopt any spiritual ceremony if they so desire.*

To make sure that the project succeeds in all its Phases, it has been proposed that all traditional Indians joining and participating in the project take the pledge of allegiance to the Independent North American Indian State of Ganienkeh, while holding the string of sacred Pledge Wampum in hand and the following words to be used in taking the Pledge are hereby suggested:

_I_____, do pledge on the Sacred Wampum that I shall support defend and protect the Independent North American Indian State of Ganienkeh. I accept the Great Law of the Six Nations Iroquois Confederacy as the Constitution of the Independent North American Indian State of Ganienkeh and do pledge to obey its laws and to defend it to the best of my ability. I do pledge to work in the interest of all the people of the Independent North American Indian State of Ganienkeh who are engaged in developing the Indian State into an example of proper, moral government and society. I accept the co-operative economic system as the most practical and worthy of the human state and do pledge to do my full share of the work to help in its success. I pledge to co-operate fully with others who are taking this Pledge of Allegiance to the end that the people of the Independent North American Indian State of Ganienkeh may realize fully their human rights and know peace and happiness.

INDEX

Adirondack Mountains 1
Adirondack Park 1
Adirondack Park Assoc.(APA) 42
A.I.M. (American Indian
    Movement) 8,77,78
Akwesasne Notes 36
Alcatraz 9
Alcohol, Tobacco & Firearms (ATF)
    9,119
Alfred, Richard 8
American Indian 1
American Opinion Magazine 139
Attorney General 11
Banks, Dennis 8,78,140
Barnum.Barney
    56,73,74,78,88,89,123,124, 157
Barnum, Betty 37,88
Bellecourt, Clyde 8,78
Bellecourt, Vernon 8,67,78
Bennett, Bonnie 52,158
Bennett, Doug 52,101,158
Big Foot 56,
Big Brother Law 41
Big Moose Road 1,
Big Moose Lake 2,51
Biggane, James 34
Black Hills 8
Blair, Michael
    29,92,96,101,131,136,139
Blumberg, Henry 111
Bowes, Diane 89
Brandt, Joseph 7,39

Brandt Treaty 39
Brown, Grace 2
Bubb Lake Trail 122
Buckheit, Scott 98,120
Bull, Sarah Badheart 8
Buerau of Criminal Investigation
    (BCI) 53
Bureau of Indian Affairs (BIA) 8
Canandaigua Treaty 7,62
Canadian Mohawk Indians 2
Camp Defiance 71
Cary, Hugh 91
Cayugas 7
Charland, Robert 24,61,63,83,97
Chesebro, Bill 75, 97, 98,114,
    117,119,126, 127, 157
Chesebro, Ruby 157
Chester, Gregory 134
Chretien, Jean 142
Chromey, George 13,164
Cole, Butch 89
Colosi, Thomas 100
Concerned Persons of Central
    Adirondacks (COPCA) 73,
    89,90,96,100,101,111,115
Cornell University 64,65
Coulter, Tim 129
Crofoot, Bob 16, 54, 55, 69, 71,
    74,158
Cuomo, Mario 100,146
Custer, George 59
Czechoslovakia 29

Deleronde. Judy 84
Deleronde, Paul 79
DEC Offices 41,119
Dokuchitz, Peter 87,94
Donovan, James 87, 94,111
Drake, Michael 48, 51, 52, 159
Drake, Stephen48, 51, 52, 89,159
Drieser, Theodore 2
Drug Enforcement Agency (DEA) 9,
Eagle Bay 2,
Einhorn, Arthur 29
Everett, Edward 134,
Everett Report 134,
F.B.I. 119,
Fessenger, Fred 61,
Fort Stanwicks Treaty 21,
Ford, Gerald 106,
Fort Laramie Treaty 9,
Gallo, Romey 13, 31, ,37, 73, 74,78, 102, 117 118
Ganienkeh 24, 77,
Ganienkeh Manifest 21, 27
Gayanerakowa 10,
Gildersleeve, Richard 53, 59, 118
Gill. Robert 30,
Gillette, Chester 2,
Ginny 116,
Glenmore Hotel 2,
Goeman, Stoney116
Goodwin, Peter 119,
Goon Squad 8
Haley, Daniel 92
Hall, Louis 8,10, 5, 95, 97, 115, 116, 139
Herkimer County 2
Herman, Sam 111
Hiawatha 6
Hiawentha 6

Hodenasaunee
Honorary Warrior
Idlehoch, Lester 57
Interlopers 77
Iroquois,Nation 129
Isley, John 114,
Jefferson Community College
    Jochnowitz, Jeremiah John Birch
    Society 139, 140
Judson, Bill 89 Julian. Ron 117
Kakwirakeron 27
Kanawake 6, 10
Karoniaktajeh 24
Keefe, William 157
Kelly, Tom 124, 125
Kunstler, William 61,62
Lake George 1
Lake Placid 1
Lakota Sioux 8, 9
Landsman, Gail
Lazore, Mike 78
Leclair, Louis 82
Leclair, Louise 82
Lockwood, Brad 79
Long House People 4, 43
Loomis, George 54, 58, 59, 117
Lynch, Robert 130
Lyons, Oren 61
Madigan, Aprile 3,49 56, 89, 131, 149
Madigan, Jean 57
Madigan, Roger 56
Madigan, Steven 57
Marleau, Bill 22
Marshals, U.S.
Martin, Howard 89
Martin, Wayne 18, 47, 53, 58, 65
Maytag, Ann 145
McCalister, Denny 57, 89

McCumber, Donna 85
Montour, Arthur 8, 27, 36, 79, 84, 93, 97, 102, 116
Montour, Danny 84
Montour, Lorraine 84, 99
Montour, Verna
Moose River Plains 14
Morse Lake 14
Moss Lake Girls Camp 2, 6, 14, 81, 84
Mount St. Helens 9
Myers, Mike 78
Nixon, Richard 9
Oglala Sioux 8
Okinawa 132
Oneida Indians 7
Onondaga Indians 7
Paper Indians 6
Payne, Bruce 125
Pine Ridge Reservation 9
Plastic Palace 71, 73
Pollet, Ray 93
Port, Edward 129, 130
Presbyterian Church 31
Quick, Robert 130
Raquette Lake 1
Reid, Ogden 42, 99, 122
Rights For American Indians Now (RAIN) 83, 95
Riders, Jane
Riders, Robert
Saranac Lake 1
Sawantis 59
Schreck, John 52
Sears, William 87, 94, 111
Sehring. George 53
Sehring, Nancy 53
Seneca Indians 7
Six nations 8

Smith, Darle 8
Smith, Ale 52, 54, 55
Speak in Council 127,
St..Lawrence River 1,
St. Lukes Hospital 150
Stark, Elmer 94
Stearns, Nancy 129
Stillman, Lu Lu 136
Stone Hawk 118, 120
Stoney 116
Stuhlburg, Josh 100
Swamp, Jake 81
Tarbell.Bill 134
Tecumseh
Tug Hill 96,101
Town of Webb PD 14, 16. 74
Turtle Island Trust 145
Tuscarora Indians
U.S. Constitution 7
Upton, Helen 136
United Nations 132,
Vigilantes, Phantom 45
Vigilantes, Young 37, 41, 44
Wampum 97,
Wampum Belt 28,
War Chief 10,
Wasser, Martin 122,
White Feather 119,
White Danny et al 38,
White, Donald 9,
Winters, Bob 89,